W9-AMC-529

New Genetics

THE STUDY OF LIFELINES

J. S. Kidd and Renee A. Kidd

CHELSEA HOUSE
PUBLISHERS
An imprint of Infobase Publishing

This one is for Loren.

✦

New Genetics: The Study of Lifelines

Chelsea House
An imprint of Infobase Publishing
132 West 31st Street
New York NY 10001

Library of Congress Cataloging-in-Publication Data

Kidd, J. S. (Jerry S.)
    New genetics : the study of life lines / J. S. Kidd and Renee A. Kidd.
        p. cm. — (Science and society)
    Previous ed. published in 1999 under title: Lifelines: the story of the new genetics.
    Includes bibliographical references and index.
    ISBN 0-8160-5604-8
    1. Genetics—Juvenile literature. 2. Genetics—Social aspects—Juvenile literature. 3. Human genetics—Juvenile literature. 4. Human genetics—Social aspects—Juvenile literature. I. Kidd, Renee A. II. Kidd, J. S. (Jerry S.). Life lines. III. Title. IV. Science and society (Facts On File, Inc.)

    QH437.5.K53 2005
    576.5—dc22   2005040141

Chelsea House books are available at special discounts when purchased in bulk quantities for businesses, associations, institutions, or sales promotions. Please call our Special Sales Department in New York at (212) 967-8800 or (800) 322-8755.

You can find Chelsea House on the World Wide Web at http://www.chelseahouse.com

Text design by James Scotto-Lavino
Cover design by Pehrsson Design
Illustrations by Sholto Ainslie

Printed in the United States of America

MP FOF 10 9 8 7 6 5 4 3 2 1

This book is printed on acid-free paper.

Contents

Preface

The products of science and technology influence the lives of all citizens, including young adults. New means of communication and transportation, new ways of doing work and pursuing recreation, new foods and new medicines arrive almost daily. Science also engenders new ways of looking at the world and at other citizens. Likewise, science can raise concerns about moral and ethical values.

Dealing with all such changes requires some resiliency. The needed adaptations by individuals are fostered by knowledge of the inner workings of science and technology and of the researchers and engineers who do the studies and design the products. Consequently, one of the goals of the Science and Society set of books is to illuminate these subjects in a way that is both accurate and understandable.

One of the obstacles in reaching that goal is the fact that almost all the connections between citizens and scientists are impersonal. For example, the direction of study in a specialized field of science is now mainly determined by negotiations between the leaders of research projects and government officials. National elections rarely hinge on questions of science and technology. Such matters are usually relegated to secondary political status. In any case, most of the officials who are concerned with science are not elected but are appointed and are members of large government bureaucracies.

Other influences on the directions taken by science and technology come from other bureaucratic organizations, such as international political bodies, large commercial firms, academic institutions, or philanthropic foundations. However, in recent years, influence has also come from more informal voluntary groups of citizens and citizen action organizations. The scope of the set has been revised to reflect the growing importance of such channels linking citizens to the leaders in science.

The books describe some of the dramatic adventures on the part of the people who do scientific work, show the human side of science, and convey the idea that scientists experience the same kinds of day-to-day frustrations that afflict everyone.

The revisions attempt to show some of the developing trends in the impact of science on sections of the citizenry such as groupings by age or gender—or geographic location. An example is the change in the living conditions in small, rural communities that have come about as a consequence of agricultural mechanization. Finally, the books describe some of the significant strides in the actual findings of science in recent years. Some fields of science such as genetics and molecular biology have gone through a virtual revolution. These radical changes are ongoing. Likewise, the development of natural medicines was recently given social prominence by the establishment of government agencies devoted explicitly to the support of such research.

Science and Society shows the extent to which individuals can have a stake in the enterprise called science and technology—how they can cope with the societal changes entailed and how they can exert some personal influence on what is happening.

Acknowledgments

We take note of the support provided by the staff of the College of Information Studies of the University of Maryland, particularly Associate Dean Diane Barlow.

Colleagues at the Commission for the Behavioral and Social Sciences and Education at the National Research Council have provided strong support. Anne Mavor, James McGee, and Susan McCutchen were especially helpful.

Lastly, researchers at the National Institute of Health and at the University of Kansas provided guidance when called upon.

Introduction

New Genetics is one of a set on the general theme of science and society. The goal of this book is to convey the social impact of modern genetic research and that of the emergent science of molecular biology. Present-day genetic discoveries offer many opportunities to improve the human condition. These discoveries point the way toward early diagnosis, disease prevention, and a variety of new treatments. These advances in knowledge are being applied to hereditary diseases such as sickle-cell anemia. New genetic information will also be used to combat the aging process and against specific conditions such as cancer and heart disease.

Farther over the horizon is the prospect of individualized health care. The possibility arises that health care providers could one day know the exact biochemical changes brought about in a particular individual by a particular disease or disability. They could then prescribe the specific molecules needed to remedy the condition with a minimum of side effects. An even more intriguing possibility is that a person's immune system could be adjusted to prevent the occurrence of any and all infectious diseases.

In addition to affecting human health, genetic techniques are being used to develop new species of plants that are resistant to frost, drought, fungal infections, and insect attack. Food crops are being improved to provide enhanced nutritional value. For example, corn kernels now contain more protein

Plant breeders and genetic engineers have produced corn that yields more than double the historic quantity. (Courtesy of the Agricultural Research Service of the U.S. Department of Agriculture)

and proportionately fewer carbohydrates than heretofore through modifications of the corn's genes.

Animals, too, can be bred to have increased nutritional value. For example, hogs are being modified to produce more lean meat and less fat. Genetic engineering is being used also to adjust animal's endocrine functions so that, for example, sheep will produce human hormones in their milk.

Most health-care professionals and medical scientists have a positive view of genetic research and biological innovation. However, some scientists and many nonscientists are concerned that the new technologies may actually threaten human health and the quality of life. While genetic screening could be an advantageous way to obtain advanced warning about a person's susceptibility to disease, for example, the same information could be misused to deny a person's employment or insurance coverage.

Many such people are also worried about potential genetic accidents. As it is possible to transfer genes from one organism into another using viruses as carriers, for example, a supposedly harmless virus could be misidentified when used as genetic carrier and serve instead as an agent of disease. In fact, such an accident nearly occurred with a virus that can cause cancer in monkeys. Genetic researchers now take elaborate precautions to prevent such an accident from happening.

Additional concerns have been raised about genetic contamination among plants. Crop plants are being genetically modified to resist the effects of herbicides. Environmentalists worry that the genes that give crop plants such resistance could be transferred to weeds. Such a transfer would mean that more intense herbicide applications would be needed to rid the fields of weeds.

In addition to considerations of medical and agricultural technology, many people worry about ethical problems that may result from tampering with human biology. For example, should parents be given the power to control the gender of their offspring? Should parents be informed of the likelihood of transmitting a disease to their unborn children? Soon, almost everyone will be confronted with questions that arise from advances in genetic science.

Major research efforts are needed to develop the genetic concepts that will yield beneficial outcomes and to identify and control genetic technologies that carry risks to health or the environment. Large portions of such research are supported by agencies of the U.S. government. One major sponsor is the Office of Science in the Department of Energy, whose interest in genetics stems from concern about nuclear radiation and mutations. Another is the National Science Foundation, which has the goal of expanding the understanding of basic biological science. Yet another major sponsor is the National Institutes of Health in the Department of Health and Human Services. The latter's interest grew from its goals of understanding both basic biology and possible health care applications. In these federal agencies, the public's interest is registered through political channels—mainly by oversight from Congress.

Substantial funding also comes from philanthropic organizations such as the Carnegie Institution and the Howard Hughes Medical Institute. Such organizations can underwrite politically sensitive projects such as stem cell research. Finally, commercial corporations invest in genetic research in the hope that knowledge gained can be sold, as such, or used in the design of marketable products such as new pharmaceuticals.

Citizen concerns about the science of genetics and its applications are most effectively represented by voluntary organizations. Some of these organizations focus on a particular disease or disease category. The Cystic Fibrosis Foundation is an example of the former and the American Cancer Society is an example of the latter. Other organizations have their focus on matters such as the quality of the environment. Their positions on public policy issues can be quite complicated. For example, some advocate the genetic modification of microbes so that the microbes can effectively consume environmental contaminants such as spilled crude oil, whereas others are wary because the modified bacteria might attack petroleum products in storage tanks. No matter the case, voluntary organizations provide a voice for citizens. That voice can be heard in testimony before congressional committees and through lobbying and contributions to political campaigns.

Citizen advocacy is most effective, however, when it is based on a solid factual foundation. This book explains how the science of genetics emerged. For centuries, humans successfully but unscientifically practiced genetics by selecting and breeding the best pets, farm animals, fruits, vegetables, trees, and flowers in order to develop desirable characteristics. Then in the mid-1800s, Gregor Mendel, an Austrian monk and village science teacher, began to study the life cycle of the flowering sweet pea plant. His painstaking investigations revealed the basic processes of genetic inheritance, and decades later, his findings began a revolution in the biological sciences. This is the story of the successive stages in that revolution and the men and women who have played crucial roles in its progress.

1

Heritage and Heredity

According to the Bible, people have long recognized that children resemble their parents. To this day, people often remark that a child is the "spittin' image" of a father, mother, or grandparent. The comment is given with a smile and the observation evokes parental pride. When parents see their features repeated in their children, they may feel a sense of continuity with the past and the future.

The Mechanics of Inheritance

Humans have long acknowledged a biological reason for the physical characteristics that are passed from generation to generation. Indeed, the biblical phrase "flesh of my flesh" suggests that some physical part from each parent has come together to form the child. However, the child is never an exact duplicate of either parent. A child may have the father's eye color and the mother's hair color. Another physical feature, such as height, may reflect a compromise between the size of the parents. Moreover, one of the child's facial features, such as the nose, may be very different from that of either parent or other close relatives. The characteristic might be a "throwback," that is, the child reveals an ancestral trait that has not been seen in recent generations. Today's geneticists can explain why such dormant traits reappear.

Early Theories

In the beginning of the 1800s, a French biologist, Jean-Baptiste Lamarck, worked out the principal ideas of biological evolution, the theory that present-day life-forms have descended from common ancestors. Mainly, his ideas made good sense. However, he also advanced some peculiar ideas on biological development and heredity. For example, he proposed that the development of new organs came about because of need, so if small, tree-dwelling animals needed to move easily from one tree limb to another or between trees some distance apart, they would develop thin folds of skin between their arms and the sides of their bodies that would allow them to form a winglike structure by stretching their arms. They could then coast from tree to tree. Lamarck believed that in this way, flying squirrels came into existence. Likewise, he asserted that traits imposed by environmental influences shaped the biological characteristics of individuals and helped influence the traits inherited by their offspring. He reasoned that when a person masters a new skill or adapts to an environmental condition, that ability is passed on to the next and successive generations.

English biologists then extrapolated Lamarck's conclusions to arrive at the misconception that individuals could enhance the inherited characteristics of their offspring by deliberately trying to improve their own capabilities. Misled plant breeders attempted to obtain new, more resilient varieties of plants by exposing parent plants to various environmental stresses, such as drought. The undertaking did not succeed and was soon abandoned.

The misguided biologists also used Lamarck's theory to explain animal appearance and behavior. They believed that ancient giraffes stretched their necks to reach the leaves high in the trees. Each generation of giraffe stretched a little more and the slightly longer necks were inherited by its offspring. Finally, giraffes' necks reached their present length.

However, evolution does not work that way. It works through a process known as natural selection, which was first explained in 1859 by Charles Darwin. Some ancestral giraffes had short necks and some had necks that were somewhat longer. During times when low branches were picked clean by insects or other animals, the shorter-necked giraffes could not find food. They did not survive long enough to reproduce and so failed to pass their traits to the next generation. However, individuals with longer necks could eat the high, leafy food that the others could not reach. Therefore, the longer-necked individuals would be well fed and have a better chance of reproducing. Their offspring would inherit the long necks of their parents. The neck length, however, was an inherited trait, not an acquired one. Acquired traits cannot be inherited.

Some individuals are adversely affected by their inherited traits. The discomfort experienced by hay fever sufferers is an example of the negative consequences of a genetic adaptation. The victims' genetic programs direct their bodies to treat airborne plant pollen as harmful microscopic invaders. The person suffers from a runny nose and eyes, sneezing, coughing, and other unpleasant complications. These behaviors are part of a genetic program to help a victim fight infections such as a cold or the flu. However, in the case of hay fever, no infection exists, and the person suffers from the body's misdiagnosis.

The Emergence of New Species

Biological evolution is based on the interaction of two factors: natural variation and some form of stress. The forms of stress come from a wide variety of sources such as epidemics, accidents, and climate changes. Natural variations are the dissimilarities found among individuals from the same species.

Natural variation within one species can be extensive. Dogs provide a good example of such wide variation. Even dogs as different as the Great Dane and the Mexican hairless are members of the same species. The reason that new species have not arisen from such different varieties is that domestic animals are shielded from environmental stresses and their breeding is usually under human control. If left in the wild, subject to natural stresses, it is likely that those variations that provided a benefit—that is, made it more likely that the dog would live to reproduce—would be passed on to more offspring. Eventually, over generations, a new species might emerge.

Early Human Intervention

For hundreds of years, humans have intervened in animal mating so as to produce domesticated animals with unusual capabilities. The mule is the product of interbreeding between a horse and a donkey. It was first described about 1000 B.C., and early mules probably resulted from accidental matings. However, humans soon recognized the virtues of such an animal and hoped to manipulate its reproduction. Mules showed the endurance and sure-footedness of a donkey and the size and strength of a horse. Humans wanted to increase the numbers of such useful animals, but there was a problem. A mule is sterile and cannot reproduce with any animal, including another mule.

The mule is an example of very rare cross-species mating. Apparently donkeys and horses are just close enough in their genetic relationship so that they can produce live offspring. The catch is that only one generation is permitted.

Humans have long used nonscientific and unsystematic ways to breed animals. In the early 1700s, the attempts became more precise and systematic. Racehorse breeding became a specialized occupation, and records began to be kept that documented the identity of the parents of each foal. Breeders mated animals with desirable and unique characteristics. They hoped that breeding two good parents would produce an even better colt whose superior traits would be passed on to successive generations.

Although breeding efforts were increasingly systematic and well organized, these informal experiments were not scientific. The breeders neither fully understood nor controlled the procedures. If the result of a breeding attempt was not successful, they just tried another approach.

During this period, many people became involved in the work of selective breeding. Wealthy landowners and professional breeders developed unusual varieties of sheep, goats, pigs, horses, dogs, and cattle. The new creatures caught the interest of the public. Professional and amateur breeders recorded their breeding techniques and often wrote magazine articles about their ideas. They advertised and sold their popular animals. Selective breeding had become both beneficial and profitable.

These successes encouraged horticulturalists (plant breeders) to try similar methods. They bred plants to obtain flowers, vegetables, and trees with new and unusual characteristics. These experiments, like those with animals, were not done in a scientific manner. For example, some horticulturalists believed that most or all traits were inherited from only the female parent.

The plant breeders, the animal breeders, and Darwin and Lamarck did not know the actual means by which inheritance worked. There was no basis for evaluating the influence of environmental factors. A scientific approach to plant and animal breeding did not appear until the late 1800s. The research of a modest Austrian monk named Gregor Mendel gave scientists the key to that mystery.

2
How Heredity Works

At the beginning of the 1800s, scientific research was not a salaried position. It was more like a hobby. Therefore, research was pursued by people with inherited wealth or by people such as teachers or clergymen, whose work allowed them free time to study the natural world. Gregor Mendel, for example, conducted botanical research during his leisure hours. Those investigations initiated the science of genetics.

Mendel was born in Moravia, a region that today forms part of the Czech Republic, in 1822. His parents, Anton and Rosine Mendel, named him Johann. The couple owned a small farm, which provided an adequate living for them and their three children. Johann, the middle child, was a sturdy youngster and enjoyed learning about his father's orchard, meadows, and farmland.

In 1843, after completing secondary school and two years of higher education, Mendel entered an Augustinian monastery near Brünn, the capital of Moravia, and took the name Gregor. There, Mendel finished his education in philosophical subjects and began his training for the priesthood. Mendel was ordained a priest in 1847.

From the first, Mendel was uncomfortable with many of his parish duties. He was often depressed by visiting the sick and dying. After two unhappy years, he found work as an unlicensed teacher of Greek and mathematics in the local high school. When Mendel attempted to qualify as a licensed teacher, he did not pass the biology and geology exams.

In 1851, the head of his monastery sent Mendel to study zoology, botany, mathematics, physics, and chemistry at the University of Vienna in Austria. After three years of advanced work, he returned to Brünn and taught natural science in the local high school. He retained this position until he was elected abbot (leader) of his monastery in 1868. Mendel was a good and efficient administrator and continued as abbot until his death in 1884.

Strangely, Mendel never gained a teaching license. He was unable to pass the science examinations. Some historians suggest that he failed because of his stubborn determination to defend his own ideas.

In 1856, Mendel began his studies on garden peas and used the monastery garden as the site of his research. During the experiments, he continued to teach his science courses at the high school. Luckily, the extensive monastery library was able to supply the necessary books on botany and other scientific subjects. Mendel also extended his knowledge by buying newly published works on science.

Although Mendel was working alone, he was encouraged by a closely knit group of local science teachers and amateur scientists. Plant breeding and animal breeding were popular ventures in the mid-1800s when Mendel began his investigations. His youthful experiences on the family farm had stimulated his curiosity about plant breeding and provided practical background for his botanical research. He was seeking methods to control the outcome of crossbreeding.

The Research

The garden pea was an ideal choice for Mendel's experiments. Pea plants are small and inexpensive, grow quickly, and are

Gregor Mendel discovered the scientific principles of inheritance from his study of sweet pea plants after crossbreeding them. (Courtesy of the National Library of Medicine)

easily available in a number of varieties. Most important, the varieties of plants can be chosen to display clearly contrasting characteristics. During his research on garden peas, he studied seven pairs of characteristics. These included smooth and wrinkled seeds, yellow and green seeds, green and yellow pods, and long and short stems.

Pea plants usually self-fertilize. Self-fertilization occurs when the female part of a plant receives pollen from the male part of the same plant. Therefore, the new plant usually has exactly the same characteristics as the parent plant.

However, peas can be artificially cross-pollinated. In this case, the pollen from one plant fertilizes a different plant. The offspring receive characteristics from each parent. During his investigations, Mendel cross-fertilized thousands of plants.

When Mendel began his research program, he chose 22 varieties of garden peas that exhibited well-defined and contrasting characteristics. For the first few years, he bred the peas to assure pure, self-fertilized strains. Thus, his rigorous experimentation began with plants whose offspring were always exactly like their parents.

The next phase of his work involved removing the pollen-bearing (male) part of each purebred plant so that there could be no self-fertilization. The pollen from one variety of pea was then used by Mendel to fertilize another variety. He crossbred pea plants with distinctly different characteristics, such as smooth seeds and wrinkled seeds. After the crossbred plants produced seeds, they were planted. In a few weeks, the new pea plant was grown to maturity and new pea pods formed and ripened. When fully ripe, the peas were harvested, examined, labeled, and placed in separate containers.

In Mendel's first experiments, he crossbred plants with smooth and wrinkled seeds. The plants of the first crossbred generation, called F1, all produced seeds with smooth coats. He was surprised by the outcome. He had expected to harvest a mixture of smooth seeds, wrinkled seeds, and seeds with partially wrinkled coats. At that time, scientists and breeders believed that crossbreeding would produce a blend or mixture of parental traits.

To continue the investigation, Mendel planted these smooth seeds of F1 to achieve the second crossbred generation, called F2. When the plants matured, the seeds were once again harvested, examined, labeled, counted, and stored. All of the seeds resembled one grandparent or another: of the 7,324 seeds harvested for this experiment, 5,474 seeds were smooth and 1,850 were wrinkled. None showed a blending of the two characteristics. Although the first generation of cross-fertilized plants had produced all smooth seeds, wrinkled seeds had reappeared in the second generation. Mendel found that there was one wrinkled seed for every three smooth seeds.

Interpretation of the Results

In the case of seed-coat texture, Mendel reasoned that each parent contributes one factor, either a smooth-coat factor or a wrinkled-coat factor. Since each seed exhibited only one characteristic, the two parental factors were in competition. Mendel termed the characteristic that appeared after the first crossbreeding the *dominant* character. The factor that disappeared after the first crossbreeding was termed the *recessive* character.

Mendel studied each pair of contrasting characteristics. In each pair, one factor was clearly dominant and one was recessive. For example, his research found yellow to be the dominant seed color and green to be the recessive one. After determining the dominant character in each pair of factors, he looked at combinations of pairs, such as seed-coat texture and seed-coat color. His early mathematical analysis proved valid when testing more than one characteristic: in any crosses between pairs of factors, only one in 16 of the second generation would show the presence of *both* recessive conditions.

Mendel's findings concerned plant heredity. Although more complicated, the transference of human eye color tends to follow the same general pattern. The brown-eyed factor is dominant. If each parent is brown-eyed and from a brown-eyed family (brown-brown), all their children will be brown-eyed. If both parents are brown-eyed but one is brown-brown and the other is from a family with both brown- and blue-eyed members (brown-blue), all their children will still be brown-eyed. However, if both parents are brown-blue, the parents will have brown eyes, but they could have blue-eyed children. Each one of those children has a one-in-four chance of having blue eyes. If both parents have blue eyes, it is likely that all their children will have blue eyes or a slight variant, such as gray eyes.

Communication

In 1865, Mendel presented his work on plant heredity to his friends in Brünn. He proposed that there was a single hereditary factor controlling each characteristic of an offspring. He speculated that the controlling factor had a physical presence—that it physically existed in both the seed and the pollen of the parents.

His talk did not generate much interest. The next year, Mendel's report was published in a scientific journal, and he sent copies to some noted German botanists. The botanists did not recognize the significance of his research. In particular, his use of mathematical analysis was not understood by his fellow botanists. Indeed, few of those botanists used any numerical calculations in their investigations during that period.

Three years after his findings were published, Mendel was elected head of the monastery and stopped his study of garden peas. His writings were quickly forgotten, and 35 years passed before they were rediscovered. Mendel died in 1884 unaware that he had founded a new discipline, the science of genetics.

Modern Botany Begins

By the late 1800s, scientific research had become a professional occupation. Well-paid people were working in government and industrial research laboratories. Professors at colleges and universities were encouraged to become involved in more research projects. Scientists were now competing for good investigative jobs. The best were often given to those with a high degree of knowledge in both science and advanced mathematics.

New and improved scientific equipment, such as more powerful microscopes, also became available to researchers. Chemists developed new dyes that could enter a living cell and stain specific structures within them. With the help of these new microscopes, scientists could see specific cellular features, such as the nucleus, a distinctive structure in the center of some cells. When the cells were treated with dye, scientists could observe strange, deeply stained strands of material inside the cell nucleus. The strands consistently absorbed so much dye that they became known as chromosomes. This name was derived from *chrôma,* the Greek word for "color," and *sôma,* another Greek word that means "body."

With the aid of a microscope, scientists could observe chromosomes during cell division in a relatively large, single-cell animal like the amoeba. First, the chromosomes duplicated themselves. The enlarged assembly of chromosomal material then separated into two identical clusters. The clusters moved to opposite sides of the cell. Finally, the parent cell split into two cells. Each of the new cells, called daughter cells, contained a full set of chromosomes. These sets were identical to the chromosomal material in the parent cell.

By 1885, most researchers concluded that the splitting and regrouping of the strands of chromosomes might indicate that this material carried the controlling hereditary factors from one generation to the next. It became clear that a physical structure existed in which hereditary information could be carried. Mendel's idea that a physical particle carrying specific information about a particular characteristic such as eye color became acceptable.

Experimental Breeding

During the 1890s, a Dutch scientist named Hugo de Vries was doing crossbreeding studies on the primrose plant. Born in 1848, he completed his university studies in Germany and returned to Holland in 1871. De Vries accepted a teaching job at the University of Amsterdam and by 1889, was well known in scientific circles for his studies of the inner workings of plant cells.

By 1889, de Vries had developed a theory of heredity. His theory stated that each trait, or characteristic, of an offspring was determined by a factor passed on by a parent. However, de Vries was uncertain about the method of interaction between the sets of parental factors. He began to experiment with garden plants to solve this mystery. De Vries's investigations led him to the

left: Hugo de Vries promoted Mendel's ideas and thereby increased interest in the scientific study of inheritance. (Courtesy of the National Library of Medicine) *bottom: De Vries first studied the wild primrose; however, the plant has erratic patterns of inheritance that led to ambiguous findings.* (Courtesy of the Agricultural Research Service of the U.S. Department of Agriculture)

De Vries later chose domesticated primrose plants to study inheritance patterns that were more orderly. (Courtesy of the National Library of Medicine)

writings of other scientists who were interested in heredity. Among these earlier writings, he found the 35-year-old paper by Gregor Mendel.

Mendel had solved the puzzle of how the factors from one parent worked with the factors from the other parent. Since this was one of the major problems that had been troubling de Vries, he was happy to find Mendel's report. He soon began promoting Mendel's results around the world. As Mendel's research became known, other scientists told of their own work on heredity. In fact, two lesser-known research scientists, Carl Correns and Erich von Tschermak, independently rediscovered Mendel's report at about the same time (in 1890). By this time, scientific advances allowed Mendel's work to be understood and appreciated by the whole scientific community.

3
Thomas Hunt Morgan and His Fruit Flies

Mendel's ideas, as publicized by de Vries, generated a flurry of activity among researchers who were studying heredity and related subjects. The microscopic study of the chromosome took on new meaning. It seemed possible to correlate the minute physical features of chromosomes with specific traits that appeared in successive generations.

The intense study of the microscopic features of plant and animal cells revealed that the chromosomes had some peculiar properties. For example, they were always to be found in the nucleus of the cell if they could be seen at all. However, when the cell was about to divide, the number of chromosomes in the nucleus doubled and the wall of the nucleus broke down so that the chromosomes entered the main body of the cell.

Using their microscopes, biologists also saw that different species had different numbers of chromosomes. For example, humans have 46 chromosomes while fruit flies have eight. Furthermore, the number of chromosomes was always even. This fact led to the idea that the chromosomes came in matched pairs. That was confirmed by looking at the arrangements of chromosomes at the time of cell division.

Morgan

Thomas Hunt Morgan was one of the research scientists studying heredity to make the most progress in genetics over a 40-year span from 1903 to 1943. His work would associate specific traits with specific locations on chromosomes, leading to a Nobel Prize for Morgan.

Morgan, whose parents were members of noted southern families, was born in 1866 in Lexington, Kentucky. He received his Ph.D. in 1890 from Johns Hopkins University in Baltimore and the next year joined the faculty of Bryn Mawr College near Philadelphia. His time was spent teaching, visiting European research stations, and writing. In 1904, he accepted a position in the department of zoology at Columbia University in New York City. Morgan remained at Columbia until 1928 when he was named head of the department of biology at the California Institute of Technology in Pasadena.

Morgan was a brilliant thinker but always seemed to be a bit disorganized. His office was usually in disarray and filled with a jumble of books and papers. Morgan was constantly thinking of new ideas. He discussed these concepts with his students, mulled them over carefully, and eventually discarded all but a few.

Morgan had a warm personality, and he inspired great loyalty from his students and colleagues. He and his students worked long hours on tedious tasks such as readying specimens to be viewed under a strong magnifying glass or microscope.

Focus on Fruit Flies

By the early 1900s, Morgan had established himself as an outstanding biologist and in 1903 became committed to testing Mendelian ideas. At the beginning of his research program, he was very skeptical of ideas such as dominance.

His decision to use fruit flies rather than Mendel's garden peas proved to have a double advantage. First, fruit flies multiply quickly. In a few days, each new generation moves from eggs to larva to sexually mature adults that mate and produce another generation. Thus, each experiment conducted by Morgan's team in their "fly room" at Columbia University required only a few weeks. Botanists working with garden plants needed months or even years to complete similar programs of study. Second, fruit flies have only four pairs of chromosomes so that analysis of chromosome features was relatively straightforward. Soon, more powerful microscopes gave Morgan another major advantage over Mendel's crude equipment. He actually saw chromosomal activity, while Mendel could only theorize about hereditary factors.

Thomas Hunt Morgan adopted Mendelian ideas after observing the patterns of inheritance of the fruit fly. (Courtesy of the National Library of Medicine)

Morgan and his team spent thousands of hours peering at their fruit flies. At first, they were looking for natural variations in the flies. Morgan realized that Mendel's peas exhibited many contrasting traits, but almost all fruit flies are identical. Morgan needed to find contrasting traits among his population of fruit flies so that he could track the differences through successive generations. Eventually, they found a male fly with white eyes rather than the normal red eyes. When this fly was bred with a normal red-eyed female, the male offspring had white eyes, and the female offspring had red eyes. This finding did not agree with Mendelian ideas. It led, however, to an important new concept.

The fly room workers had already found that one of the four chromosome pairs of the fruit fly came in two varieties. Females always had two full-sized chromosomes in the fourth pair. Males had one full-sized chromosome and one shrunken chromosome in that fourth set. They deduced that gender was dictated by this difference. They designated the large gender chromosome as the X chromosome and the small gender chromosome as the Y chromosome.

Since the white eye mutation always was associated with male gender, it seemed likely that a natural mutation had taken place on the stunted male chromosome. A mutation is an alteration of the chromosome, which often causes a change in the appearance or function of an organism. This association of gender and eye color led to the introduction of a theory called "linkage." In its initial formulation, the theory stated that some specific characteristics are always transmitted to males, while others are always passed on to females.

After finding one spontaneous mutation, the fly room workers were anxious to find others. However, the natural

A genetically mutated fruit fly that is unable to see or hear. Study of the modified gene is providing clues about the human senses.
(Courtesy of Richard Walker, University of California at San Diego)

processes of mutation proved to be too slow and too uncertain for their studies, so they looked for other means to achieve mutant fruit flies. Starting around 1910, Morgan's studies were aided by the growing body of information on mutations. By then, most scientists believed that mutations could be induced by interfering with genetic material. This interference could include radiation from X-rays or changes in the chemical environment in which the flies lived. Morgan and his coworkers began to irradiate their fruit flies. When changes occurred in the adult animal, they often could be connected to visible changes in the chromosomes.

The ability to induce mutations, and to see the resulting changes in both the chromosomes and the flies' physical characteristics, helped Morgan and his students find the particular location on a chromosome that carried a particular trait. These additional microscopic examinations of the chromosomes led them to expand the theory of linkage to all the chromosomes. In other words, it was established that each chromosome carried a particular set of characteristics, each of which had its own location on the chromosome.

In 1909, a Danish biologist named William Johannsen coined a word for the little understood—and at that time invisible—units that carry all hereditary information. The determiner became known as a *gene,* from the Greek word meaning "birth" or "origin." By 1910 it was widely believed by scientists that the genes were associated with the chromosomes. The idea of the gene fit well into the thoughts of those who worked in the fly room. However, neither Johannsen nor any other biologist could determine how a tiny segment of microscopic chromosome was able to carry all the necessary information to transmit a particular trait. While Morgan explored his concept of linkage, he continued to examine the relationship between chromosomes and specific hereditary factors. Because of their intense concentration on the physical form of the chromosomes, Morgan and his

Crossing Over

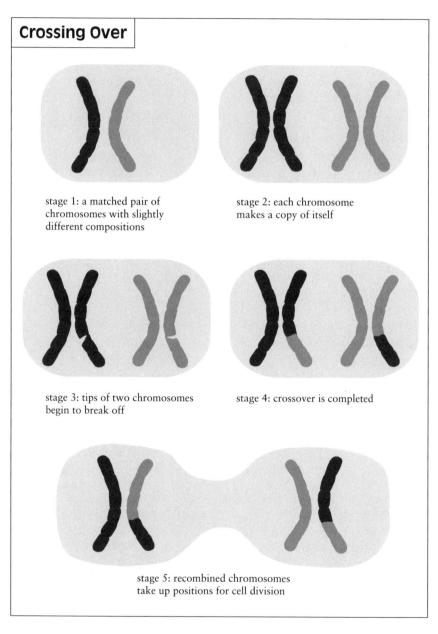

stage 1: a matched pair of chromosomes with slightly different compositions

stage 2: each chromosome makes a copy of itself

stage 3: tips of two chromosomes begin to break off

stage 4: crossover is completed

stage 5: recombined chromosomes take up positions for cell division

This schematic drawing of a pair of fruit fly chromosomes shows an example of the crossing over of genetic material.

students observed several extraordinary processes that no one had seen before. Among the most important advances made by Morgan and his team was an understanding of the "crossover" that takes place in reproductive cells, an egg cell or a sperm cell. In a crossover, matching segments in a pair of chromosomes break off and change places; in other words, they cross over from one chromosome of the pair to the other. As a result of crossover, the chromosomes passed on to children are reshuffled versions of the chromosomes inherited from parents. When children in the same family strongly resemble one another, there has been little crossover in the chromosomes of the reproductive cells. When brothers and sisters look very different, chromosomal crossover has probably been extensive.

Continuing research on crossover helped refine the concept of linkage. The relative location of a particular gene on a chromosome was established by first showing that two traits that crossed over in the same generation had to be controlled by genes that were physically close together on the chromosome. In other words, if two traits were seen together over several generations, it meant that they were probably on the same arm of a particular chromosome.

If, after many hundreds of generations, the traits continue to appear together, it is probable that the genes for these traits are close together on the same chromosome. By looking at many generations, it was possible to estimate closely how far apart on a chromosome any given trait was from any other trait.

These investigations led to the first crude maps of where genes are located on a chromosome. Over several generations through which several different traits were traced, the location of specific genes could be shown to be arranged like beads on a string.

While at Columbia University from 1904 to 1928, Morgan and his students produced a large body of important research.

Many of his students went on to become world-famous research scientists. In 1928, Morgan accepted an administrative position in the biology department of the California Institute of Technology in Pasadena. Before his death in 1945, he received many awards, including the Nobel Prize in physiology or medicine in 1933.

4

Magic Places— Productive People

By the early 1900s, independent research was no longer a common practice because scientists needed the facilities and financial support of large institutions. Hugo de Vries conducted his research at the University of Amsterdam. Thomas Hunt Morgan worked at Columbia University in New York City. Many famous institutions, such as Johns Hopkins University in Baltimore; Cornell University in Ithaca, New York; the University of Illinois in Champaign; and the California Institute of Technology in Pasadena, were important centers for the development of genetic science.

Woods Hole and Cold Spring Harbor

Two lesser-known institutions, the Marine Biological Laboratory at Woods Hole, Massachusetts, and the Station for Experimental Evolution near Cold Spring Harbor in New York, played major parts in the history of genetics. Neither of these facilities is associated with a college or university.

The Marine Biology Laboratory at Woods Hole was organized in 1896 and began operation in 1898. The facility was founded by the Woman's Educational Society of Boston to acquaint local high school and college biology teachers with new research techniques. The training sessions were scheduled during the summer holidays.

The program soon grew beyond this modest plan. Many famous biologists began coming to Woods Hole every summer. The scientists and their families liked the seashore and the cool ocean breezes. Most of all, however, the scholars liked the chance to work full-time on research and share thoughts and ideas with their colleagues.

In 1902, Thomas Hunt Morgan stayed at Woods Hole during his summer vacation from Bryn Mawr College. He soon encouraged other outstanding biologists such as Jacques Loeb and Edmund Beecker Wilson to join him at the beach. During the summers between 1910 and 1925, Morgan conducted many of his groundbreaking fruit fly studies. During the first 10 years, the number of summer visitors increased rapidly. Both work space and living space at Woods Hole were soon in short supply.

From the first day the facility was open, operating funds were also in short supply. As early as 1901, some considered inviting the University of Chicago to take charge of the laboratory and create a branch campus at Woods Hole. This idea was rejected. The administrators of Woods Hole wanted the facility to stay independent.

In 1902, shortly after the Woods Hole trustees decided to remain independent, the Carnegie Institution of Washington, offered to fund the laboratory. The Carnegie people wanted to exclude students and hire full-time researchers who would use all the space and equipment on a year-round basis. This proposal was also rejected. However, the Carnegie Institution did help finance the work at Woods Hole with $10,000 donations for each of the next three years. Other philanthropic organizations later provided both endowment and operating funds.

Andrew Carnegie, the founder of the institution, was interested in advancing basic scientific research such as the work done at Woods Hole. Carnegie was born in Scotland in 1835. When he was 13 years old, he and his parents moved to the United States. Starting as an unskilled factory worker in western Pennsylvania, Carnegie became a millionaire in the iron and steel business. He formed the United States Steel Company in 1901 and soon turned his attention from business to philanthropy. His most famous patronage concerned the construction of hundreds of public libraries and the founding of the Carnegie Institute of Technology—now Carnegie Mellon University—and the Carnegie Institution of Washington.

The Carnegie Institution was created in 1902 from an organization called the Washington Memorial Institute, which had been established by a group of women who hoped to found a national university in Washington, D.C. After this idea was rejected by some federal politicians, the women determined to develop a learning center where students from around the country could spend a semester or a year in Washington, D.C. The students would study at the Library of Congress, the Smithsonian Institution, and other regional facilities. The idea was accepted by Andrew Carnegie's advisers and funding was approved.

Soon, however, the advisers began to change the original concept. Ultimately, the aims of the Carnegie Institution were quite dissimilar from those proposed by the women of the Washington Memorial Institute. The advisers decided to create a permanent installation for senior research scientists. Visiting students were not permitted to use the facility.

The administrators of the new Carnegie Institution hoped to found other research laboratories. When they could not acquire the property at Woods Hole, they decided to build their own facilities. Soon, they built a marine biology laboratory on Loggerhead Key, an island in the Gulf of Mexico off the coast of Florida. Then in 1904, the institution founded the Station for Experimental Evolution, located near the village of Cold Spring Harbor on Long Island Sound.

The early history of Cold Spring Harbor is similar to that of Woods Hole. Both facilities had been originally planned as summer schools. John D. Jones, a wealthy New York merchant, wanted to support higher education on Long Island. When the Brooklyn Institute of Arts and Sciences sought his help in 1890, Jones donated land and provided money for a summer school with extensive laboratories. He donated another piece of his property to the state of New York for a fish hatchery. Before his death in 1895, Jones established a trust to oversee his generous gifts.

In 1903, representatives of the Carnegie Institution approached the trustees with a plan to share the laboratory resources at Cold Spring Harbor. A year later, people from the Brooklyn Institute and the Carnegie Institution were jointly involved with the founding of the Station for Experimental Evolution.

This shared venture continued until 1924 when the Brooklyn Institute withdrew from the arrangement. The Carnegie Institution and the Long Island Biological Association (LIBA), a local citizen organization founded by Jones, then began a cooperative undertaking at Cold Spring Harbor.

By 1960, it was evident that new arrangements were needed. Biological research was expanding rapidly, and the Carnegie trust could not fund the necessary laboratory improvements. The Carnegie Institution suggested the possibility of government funding, but the administrators of LIBA were against becoming dependent on government money. Consequently, the Carnegie Institution withdrew from the entire venture in 1963.

Fortunately, Cold Spring Harbor was renowned for the high quality of its research and teaching. The laboratory was able to attract financial support from many sources. Regional universities, private foundations, large corporations, government agencies, and local individuals all stepped in. Cold Spring

Harbor Laboratory was able to remain an independent research institution.

The Genetics of Corn

In 1906, George Shull, a young geneticist, began his research at Cold Spring Harbor. He was interested in the work of Hugo de Vries, who had rediscovered the work of Gregor Mendel. At first, Shull paralleled de Vries's investigations by studying the primrose. Soon, however, he decided to experiment with corn.

Shull established two purebred lines of corn plants—line A and line B. All line A plants descended from one parent plant. All line B plants from another. In corn plants, each kernel on an ear of corn is an egg, which is fertilized by a different grain of pollen. To achieve purebred plants, all the corn kernels on an ear of corn must be fertilized by pollen from the same plant. In corn breeding, this process is called selfing, or self-fertilization.

Shull enclosed each newly formed, unfertilized ear of corn in a small paper bag. When an ear had developed, the bag was opened. A tassel from the same plant was carefully removed from the stalk. The tassel is the uppermost, male portion of the plant. The pollen on the tassel was shaken above the ear of corn to fertilize the kernels. The bag was then resealed to prevent future pollination. This procedure was repeated to self-fertilize all the kernels on each ear of corn. The mature kernels of this self-fertilized corn were the seeds for the next generation of purebred plants.

The initial results were very strange. Instead of the vigorous plants seen in the earlier research on self-fertilization of the garden pea, Shull's corn plants were stunted and unhealthy in appearance. After being inbred for eight generations, the sickly, pure lines were crossed. Plants from line A were interbred with those of line B. The pollen from one line was used to fertilize the kernels of the other. The results were astonishing. The corn plants obtained from line AB were amazingly vigorous and productive. The resultant agricultural product is known as hybrid corn. The exact nature of hybrid vigor is still not well understood. However, by the use of hybrid seed, productivity levels have increased by 10 to 20 percent compared to the yields from ordinary, cross-fertilized field corn.

Shull's major advance in crop breeding resulted from his interest in genetic theory. He had no concern for the practical application of his findings and returned to basic scientific research. Shull next sought to discover how a seed can contain enough information to direct the complete formation of an adult plant. Other agricultural scientists continued his investigations and succeeded in producing large volumes of hybrid seed.

Barbara McClintock

The research facility at Cold Spring Harbor was home to another important geneticist, Barbara McClintock. McClintock was to make major discoveries about genes' ability to move between chromosomes.

McClintock was born in 1902 in the state of Massachusetts. Her father was a physician, and her mother was a member of a well-established New England family. McClintock was the third child of the McClintocks' four children. When her younger brother was born, she was sent to live with her father's relatives. After she returned home, McClintock did not enjoy a close relationship with her parents. She developed an independent spirit that guided her future life.

When McClintock was 16 years old, she enrolled in the College of Agriculture at Cornell University in Ithaca, New

York. Her mother objected to this decision, but her father supported her goals.

In the 1920s, Cornell was unusual because women were welcomed into undergraduate and graduate science programs. At that time, only Cornell and the University of Chicago gave such educational opportunities to women. Cornell had another uncommon feature that appealed to McClintock. The agriculture college was one of the first schools to use government funding for free tuition.

McClintock enjoyed college life and the people she met. She liked her courses, especially those in biology. In her junior year, she was invited to enroll in a graduate-level genetics course. For the first time, McClintock became involved with scientific research.

McClintock's work was of a high caliber, and she was allowed to continue her graduate-level studies in plant and animal biology. She often investigated corn plants to improve her understanding of basic biological principles. Fortunately, the faculty in the College of Agriculture was eager to support research about corn. McClintock completed her undergraduate work at Cornell and was immediately accepted into the graduate program.

In 1922, during her first year as a graduate student, McClintock learned to distinguish the tiny variations in size, shape, and striation (stripes) in the various chromosomes of the corn plant. With her assistance, some of the sharper-eyed professors and fellow students were able to see these elements. Luckily, McClintock's fine drawings allowed all of her colleagues to envision the striations and other important characteristics. For the next 11 years, McClintock's research on the corn plant was the best source of information on the structure of chromosomes, the workings of the individual cell, and the formation of the mature organism.

During her graduate research, McClintock frequently worked with Indian corn. This type of corn has kernels in a

Barbara McClintock carried out intensive studies of the germinal cell of corn and was able to observe exchanges of genetic material between the corn chromosomes. (Courtesy of the Carnegie Institution of Washington, D.C.)

variety of colors. With a microscope, McClintock could observe that small variations in chromosome structure correspond with the colors of the kernels. These color-coded variations were an interesting and beautiful example of genetics at work.

McClintock received her doctoral degree in 1927. She accepted an instructorship at Cornell and continued her research. Her work on corn chromosomes focused on an investigation of linkage groups. Each of these groups is a cluster of traits or characteristics that are always linked together and inherited as a group. As an example, brown kernels, stripped leaves, and short tassels are found together in a corn plant. Earlier fruit fly studies had shown that an understanding of linkage was helpful in controlling the results of crossbreeding. McClintock reasoned that the new hybrid corn industry would benefit from this scientific approach to breeding.

McClintock knew a great deal about corn chromosomes, but she had no practical experience in breeding and raising corn. Luckily, she found two graduate students to assist her, Marcus Rhoades and George Wells Beadle. Both became renowned scientists. After Rhoades graduated from Cornell, he taught genetics at Columbia University, the University of Illinois, and the University of Indiana. While a respected geneticist in his own right, Rhoades was McClintock's spokesperson for many years. McClintock's style of writing was frequently difficult to understand, and Rhoades was able to make her message more intelligible to other scientists and to the public.

Beadle grew up in the corn fields of Nebraska and understood the practical aspects of corn production. Like McClintock, he became an outstanding research scientist. In 1958, Beadle won the Nobel Prize in physiology or medicine for his work in genetics.

McClintock's three-member team soon expanded to seven people. The group collaborated closely on all phases of their research. McClintock's team attracted the interest of other scientists. In 1931, Thomas Hunt Morgan, then working at the California Institute of Technology in Pasadena, delivered a lecture at Cornell. Afterward, the famed geneticist visited the biology laboratories and questioned the students about their work. Morgan learned that McClintock and a new graduate student named Harriet Creighton were investigating his theory on linkage and crossover. McClintock and Creighton had determined that crossover of chromosomal material was commonplace and that such crossovers sometimes involved non-paired chromosomes. Morgan urged them to publish their findings. He wrote to the editor of *Science* magazine and recommended that the report be included in the next issue. Morgan was gratified that McClintock and Creighton had investigated and confirmed one of his theoretical ideas.

Between 1931 and 1933, McClintock was moving back and forth from Cornell to other sites. She was involved with a variety of short-term projects at the University of Missouri in Columbia and the California Institute of Technology. While at Missouri, she used X-rays to produce mutations in corn. This technique allowed McClintock to observe the new traits caused by deliberate genetic mutations in much the same way that Morgan had with fruit flies.

During the same period, McClintock detected a previously unknown activity of chromosomal matter that can take place during the division of corn cells. While the cell divides and crossover can be taking place, a segment of chromatin, the material that makes up a chromosome, may be torn from the chromosome. Such torn segments often form into the shape of a ring. This shape blocks the function of the genes that were split from the chromosome and enclosed in the circle. When this occurs, the offspring do not show the traits governed by the genes enclosed in the ring.

McClintock made another very important discovery in 1932. She found that one segment of a specific corn chromosome could move from one position on the chromosome to different positions either on the same chromosome or on another chromosome. She likened this bit of chromatin to the director or choreographer of a ballet. She saw that the segment controlled the movement of the other chromatin and the development of specialized cells. McClintock theorized that this tiny piece of chromatin contained either one or very few genes working together. Because of their ability to roam, these elements came to be called "jumping genes."

The study encouraged other scientists to further investigate the relationships between genetics and developmental biology and particularly the process that directs the growth and specialization of cells. Geneticists sought to determine why cells with identical chromosomes form different parts of a plant. The complete answer to this mystery is still undetermined.

In 1934, McClintock was awarded a modest Rockefeller Foundation grant and resumed her work at Cornell. However, McClintock's productivity was low, and she became depressed. She was concerned that her career ambitions would never be realized. At that time, few women scientists were offered permanent, full-time research positions.

Two years later, McClintock was invited back to the University of Missouri to work on another Rockefeller-sponsored project. Although a member of a team, McClintock worked alone on the project. During that time, she began to organize her own ideas on the development of plant and animal cells.

McClintock was unhappy during her stay at the University of Missouri. She believed that her male colleagues wanted to direct her research strategy. Although her work was well regarded, university administrators made it clear that she did not conform to their idea of a conventional woman scientist. She resigned her appointment in 1941 and set out to find a more congenial situation.

Her old friend, Marcus Rhoades, suggested that McClintock spend the summer doing research at Cold Spring Harbor. She enjoyed the working conditions but left in November when her money ran low. The next month another old friend, Milislav Demerec, was named director of the facility. He invited her to return as a resident scientist. After careful consideration, she accepted his offer and remained at Cold Spring Harbor for the rest of her working life.

Over the next 10 years, McClintock expanded her understanding of the process that controls the activities within each plant and animal cell. She believed that the repositioning of chromatin within the chromosome is responsible for key aspects of cell development. She called this process "transposition." By 1951, McClintock had determined that cellular action moves segments of chromosome through a series of steps into a final arrangement. The changes in the arrangement of chromosomal material can then be seen in the large-scale characteristics of the mature corn plant. In 1983, McClintock was awarded the Nobel Prize in physiology or medicine for this outstanding contribution to field of genetics.

The importance of her work, like that of Gregor Mendel, was slow to receive worldwide acclaim. However, McClintock was not the obscure scientist that Mendel had been. In 1939, she was elected vice president of the Genetics Society of

America. The National Academy of Sciences named McClintock a member in 1944. This is an honor granted to few individuals, male or female. The next year, she was elected president of the Genetics Society of America. In 1978, Brandeis University granted her the Rosenstiel Award, and in 1979, she received honorary degrees from Rockefeller University and Harvard University. McClintock became a MacArthur Foundation laureate in 1981. This tribute included a five-year income of $60,000 per year, tax-free. She also won the Lasher Award, the Wolf Foundation Prize, and the Horowitz Prize for Science from Columbia University. Indeed, McClintock received recognition throughout her long career.

Although McClintock was acclaimed during her lifetime, much of her research did not follow the prevailing scientific trends. During the 1920s, McClintock and other scientists were furthering George Shull's 1904 studies on the corn plant, but by the 1940s, few geneticists were interested in corn research. While an increasing number of projects were concerned with fruit flies or bacteria, McClintock continued to investigate the chromosomes of corn.

In 1938, the electron microscope was invented in Germany. The new microscopes were many times more powerful than previous models. Many theoretical elements, such as separate strands of chromosomes, could be observed for the first time. The advanced equipment reached the United States by 1944. Soon, the focus of genetic research shifted from chromosomes to genes. Most geneticists were fascinated by the prospect of being able to observe and possibly manipulate genes. The interest in chromosome research decreased sharply.

McClintock's studies had been done with an ordinary light microscope. Although she had been able to observe chromosomes, she could not see the strands of chromosomal material that held the genes. Her Nobel-winning theory of transposition had been developed without the facilitation of a high-powered microscope. During the late 1970s, geneticists realized that McClintock's concept of the movement and organization of chromatin was useful to the understanding of individual genes. McClintock's discoveries about microscopic chromosomes proved useful in the study of submicroscopic genes.

In the 1970s and 1980s, she was able to shift her energies into work with advanced students. She continued to mentor young scientists until her death at age 90 on September 2, 1992.

5

Science and Politics

People with political and economic power are sometimes tempted to oppose or distort the workings of science. This can happen when scientific findings appear to contradict a set of ideas or beliefs that have helped people with power to retain or expand that power.

True science confers no particular advantage to selected individuals or groups. The findings of true science are not produced to support any particular worldview. From time to time, however, some portion of the scientific enterprise has been captured by people of power and influence. The results of such takeovers are generally negative. At best, some losses of time and resources are incurred. Sometimes the negative consequences are more severe. Two such instances involved genetics.

Eugenics

Eugenics literally means good breeding. It is an idea that has been applied in some extremely unfortunate ways to control the mating habits and genetic assets of the human race. The success of animal and plant breeding by trial and error procedures led to speculation about the mating habits of humans. Could careful breeding of humans improve the species?

In the late 1800s, Francis Galton, a British statistician, led a movement concerned with rational human mate selection.

Galton had been impressed by some of the sweeping theories from biology and economics that were current at the time. His own studies of twins and familial bloodlines helped convince him that the human species could be improved by selective breeding in much the same way that animal species had been. However, the key to the success in the selective breeding of animals was external control over the choice of mate: the dogs, horses, cows, chickens, and so on, either male or female, had no say in the selection of a mate.

There are several obvious problems with Galton's notions. For one, no one knows exactly what traits are controlled by genes. Many studies have been undertaken to determine the role of heredity in a large number of human traits. Some of the most sophisticated researches used a method called co-twin control. The idea was to find identical twins who were raised from infancy in different environments. It was hoped that this manner of observation would allow scientists to measure the relative effects of heredity versus environment. However, after several such studies with hundreds of pairs of twins, the results are still murky. The so-called nature versus nurture debate continues.

Going further into the idea, an objection arises, tapping into basic human values. When implementing selective breeding, exactly what traits should be emphasized in mate selection? The next question is, who gets to decide—not only for trait selection but for mate selection.

A third sticking point comes from the fact that there are two strategies for control—positive and negative—and the two are not equally achievable. Positive control is the arrangement of mating based on the representation of desirable traits in one or both members of a prospective couple. Negative control is the prevention of mating by individuals who possess traits that are undesirable.

Even the most oppressive governments have never in human history been able to impose positive control over mate selection for other than a very few people, namely members of royal families. However, some forms of negative control have been put into effect. At one time in the early 1900s, individual state laws in the United States restricted the opportunity to reproduce by individuals who were judged to be mentally defective. By the 1930s, such laws had either been revoked or were generally not enforced.

In other countries, most notably in Germany, such laws were passed and extensively enforced by the dictatorial regime of Adolf Hitler. Hitler achieved total political power in Germany in 1933. His beliefs included very strong judgments about mental and physical fitness. These beliefs were linked to race or ethnicity. He sought to eliminate "negative" traits from the Germanic population by sterilizing those who did not meet his standards. He sought to eradicate sources of racial "contamination" by killing all members of ethnic minorities such as Gypsies (the Rom). One of his main targets were people of Jewish descent. He ordered that all such people be killed.

In the mid-1940s, at the end of World War II, citizens of the world were revolted by the revelations from the death camps that Hitler had built. Consequently, even those who had held views sympathetic to eugenics as a political philosophy no longer supported any form of eugenic action program that would involve human subjects.

Currently, the eugenics theories have been superseded by recognition that human behavior is not governed by a small set of genes. Instead, human capabilities arise from the combined effects of many genes in interaction with a host of factors in the person's familial and social environment. These scientific facts add weight to the belief that human pairing cannot be brought under strict control by any government or other institution. The dictatorial aspects of such a program are not in line with human values in democratic nations.

Michurin and Lysenko

Using science in an attempt to achieve political goals can generate other serious complications. A good example of this predicament is provided by events in Russia.

The drama began in 1911 when the U.S. Department of Agriculture formed a program to collect plant specimens from around the world. They sent a famous American plant expert, Frank Meyer, to Russia. He visited Kozlov, a town about 150 miles south of Moscow, to examine fruit trees bred by Ivan Michurin. Meyer was favorably impressed and returned in 1913 to purchase and ship some of the trees to the United States. During this visit, he told reporters that Michurin might be a rich man if he worked in the United States.

Michurin's Russian supporters misunderstood or distorted Meyer's remarks and used them in a propaganda campaign to make Michurin a celebrity. After the Russian Revolution in 1917, Michurin announced that if he did not receive large financial subsidies from the Soviet government, he would move to the United States. In 1922, Michurin's popular appeal caused the Soviet government to give way to his demands. Michurin's projects were subsidized for the rest of his life.

By the early 1920s, Russian agriculture was in a poor state. The Russian civil war against czarist rule had begun in 1917 and continued for several years. The Bolsheviks, members of the Communist Party, had won. The Union of Soviet Socialist Republics (USSR) was formed in early 1923. The new Soviet government soon began merging family farms into large collective farms under bureaucratic managers. Some large estates were simply taken over by the government and became "state farms." Soviet leaders believed that the larger farms would prove less expensive to operate and easier to modernize. They hoped that costly equipment such as motorized harvesting machines could be more efficiently used. These advantages did not materialize. Farm workers were demoralized and resentful.

The years of civil war and two years of drought (in 1921 and 1922) had ruined many crops in the Soviet Union. Also, the uncertain outcome of farm mergers worried many farmers.

Because of the depressed state of Russian agriculture, the leaders turned to Michurin, although many Russian scientists were skeptical about his ability. They had good reason to be. Among other dubious claims, Michurin said that the hybrid obtained from crossing a melon and a squash would retain the best properties of both plants. Michurin was incorrect, but the Soviet leaders believed his story.

Scientists were also concerned about his claims concerning fruit grown on a branch grafted to a different species of fruit tree. Grafting is a technique that allows cultivators of fruits and nuts to take advantage of the desired characteristics of each of two varieties of plants within the same species. For example, a variety of grape plants might have disease-resistant roots. Another variety might have particularly sweet and abundant fruit. The cultivator can take the fruit-bearing branches of the second variety and graft them onto the thick stems growing up from the roots of the first variety. Such grafting usually involves cutting the ends of the branches in the shape of a V. The thick stems from the root stock are cut off straight and split from the cut back toward the root for a short space. The V is inserted into the split and the junction is bound with cloth tape. More often than not, the newly attached branch will bond with the root. The resulting plant will show the properties of the two different varieties—in this case, hardy roots and abundant fruit.

Michurin stated that seeds from fruit from the grafted plant would produce offspring that exhibited characteristics from both the grafted and the host species. Although Michurin's claims were contrary to all scientific findings, he maintained that his grafting techniques allowed the transference of acquired characteristics. Soviet leaders continued to believe Michurin, and scientists refused to accept his claim. In truth, fruits grown on a grafted branch can display only the characteristics found in the plant from which the branch was taken. Neither that fruit nor its offspring can display characteristics of the host tree.

Michurin accused his critics of arrogance. He maintained that his intuition about breeding new plants was far more reliable than the prolonged experiments of overeducated, upperclass scientists. Michurin's humble background appealed to the Communist rulers who were hostile toward people from privileged backgrounds. They wanted to believe his claims. Vladimir Ilyich Lenin, who headed the Russian government after 1918, was less impressed by Michurin, but he believed that the new Soviet state would need the abilities and worldwide prestige of its scientific community and accordingly protected the scientist's interests. Even with Lenin's protection, however, colleagues were wary of Michurin's power. Their uneasiness was well founded. After Lenin died in 1924, the status of Soviet biologists became more uncertain.

By 1927, the conflicts between established biologists and Michurin began to decline. Michurin was 72 years old and beginning to withdraw from active supervision of his projects. Unfortunately, his place was soon filled by a much younger and tougher replacement, Trofim Denisovich Lysenko. Lysenko, born in 1898 into a poor farm family, was trained as an agronomist at the Kiev Agricultural Institute. Agronomy is the application of agricultural technology. His reputation was established in 1927, shortly after his graduation. He proposed that cotton fields in the southern provinces of the Soviet Union should be planted with sweet peas after the late summer cotton harvest. The relatively mild climate would allow the peas to mature before hard frosts began. The pea plants simultaneously would provide ground cover and help retain ground moisture. Cattle and other livestock could use the fields as winter pastures. In addition, the sweet pea plants would act to improve the land by putting nitrogen back in the soil.

Government officials and established agricultural technologists were impressed with Lysenko's plan. Unfortunately, this success went to his head, and he saw himself as the leading Russian agronomist.

Lysenko was severely disappointed by the rejection of his next idea, which he called the "vernalization" of winter wheat. This project involved exposing wheat seeds to cold winter weather before their planting in the early spring. Lysenko believed that an exposure to cold would ensure rapid sprouting. If so, the wheat would ripen earlier in the summer before a possible drought could damage the crop. When Lysenko presented his ideas to a scientific meeting in 1929, he was ignored. The same concept had been tested by the Ohio State Board of Agriculture in 1857—almost 70 years before. The tests showed little difference in the number of days required for sprouting to occur, and farmers were unenthusiastic about the practice.

Trofim Denisovich Lysenko holds a sample of onions aloft during a discussion about his cultivation methods. (Courtesy of the Library of Congress)

Lysenko was infuriated by the reaction of the scientists and his inability to obtain political sponsorship for his ideas. He set out to acquire enough political power to destroy his critics. This was a risky course.

He began the campaign by making exaggerated claims about his methods to increase food production. Lysenko maintained his techniques would achieve larger crops in a few years.

These claims were welcomed by high government officials such as Joseph Stalin.

After Lysenko's plans were tested, some agronomists and farm workers reported that the actual gains in crop production did not live up to the original claims. Lysenko's counterargument was simple; he said that farmers were sabotaging his program, and Stalin accepted this explanation. Lysenko remained a dominant force in Soviet agriculture until after Stalin's death in 1953.

During his almost 35 years in power, Lysenko advanced many questionable schemes. For example, some farmers in the northern areas of Russia were forced to plant corn rather than fast-maturing crops such as oats and rye. Corn needs many warm, sunny days to do well and is not a good crop for the area north of Moscow.

Lysenko refused to adopt the methods of hybridization that had been developed in the United States. These methods might have produced a variety of corn better suited to the Russian climate. However, these techniques were contrary to Lysenko's theories because they required several generations of careful inbreeding. Lysenko wanted immediate results. His supporters prevented most Soviet farmers from adopting hybrid corn until the decade before Lysenko's death in 1976.

Lysenko's high position allowed him to prohibit all genetic research in the Soviet Union. Mendel's theories and the discoveries of Morgan and other Western scientists were suppressed. Lysenko refused to accept the existence of chromosomes and genes, the carriers of all inherited traits.

Indeed, Russia continues to lag behind Europe and North America in fields such as molecular biology and genetic engineering, although Russian genetic science appears to be making a rapid recovery. Russian geneticists have been invited to team with leading scientists in an attempt to locate the human genes responsible for diseases and other medical problems.

The outcome of Lysenko's years of power prove that science and politics do not mix. Politicians cannot order a scientific investigation to fulfill a political need. Soviet leaders attempted this venture but succeeded in creating difficult and long-lasting problems. Likewise, scientists cannot distort and limit their investigations merely to promote a political agenda or to ensure personal political gains.

Since the 1950s, Soviet, and now Russian, scientists have worked to catch up to the West, particularly in the field of molecular biology. In 1959, Vladimir Engelhardt was able to establish a research center on this topic. It is presently part of the Russian Academy of Sciences. The scale of the research program, however, is still modest compared to the work going on in Europe, Japan, and North America.

6
Shifting the Research Focus

The garden pea was a good subject for early genetic research. When studying this plant, Gregor Mendel could easily identify inherited characteristics such as seed color and texture. Because of its short life cycle, the fruit fly had been Thomas Hunt Morgan's favorite research subject in the early 1900s. Investigation of the corn plant became important in the 1920s. Stronger microscopes allowed Barbara McClintock and other scientists to observe the structure and activity of chromosomes in the cells of corn. In the 1930s, interest in the fruit fly resurged when biologists discovered that the salivary gland of that insect contained large chromosomes that revealed fascinating details of structure when studied under a microscope. While progress was being made in classical genetics, parallel lines were opening up in the study of viruses and bacteria in the 1920s.

Bacteria are single-cell organisms that have no nucleus and no chromosomes. The genetic material of bacteria is in the form of loose strands and circlets called "plasmids."

Bacteria are abundant in air and soil. Most species are harmless; some are helpful such as those that transform milk into cheese; and some are harmful—causing disease.

Viruses are much smaller than bacteria and have no true cell body. They are totally parasitic in that all their sustenance and reproductive capabilities come from the cells they invade. They confiscate the resources of such cells including the host cell's ability to manufacture proteins. They are selective about the cells they invade. For example, one type of virus will attack only the cells in the leaves of a tobacco plant. Other viruses will invade selected animal cells. Within the field of genetics, interest centers on those viruses that attack bacteria.

In the 1920s and 1930s, scientists were debating the basic chemistry of genes. The majority of biologists believed that genes were made of proteins. German research begun in the 1860s revealed, however, that the cell nucleus contained a mixture of materials, not just proteins. This mixture included a substance called "nucleic acid," so named because of its location in the cell. Nucleic acid molecules appeared to be simple chains composed of sugarlike units. More specifically, to a chemist, these molecules were similar to the chains of sugar molecules that make up ordinary starch or cellulose. Few biologists believed that a simple structure such as that of nucleic acid could contain all the information needed to build a complete organism.

The Transforming Principle

In 1928, the bacteriologist Fred Griffith was studying two forms of pneumonia germs. One form had a slick outer surface, or cell membrane. The other had a rough cell membrane. When injected with the rough-coated bacteria, mice were able to fight off the infection. When injected with the slick-coated bacteria, most of the mice died. Then Griffith proceeded to look for a specific method to immunize the mice against the slick form of bacteria. While seeking a vaccine, Griffith injected mice with a mixture of slick germs they had killed using a Lysol solution and live rough germs. Most of the mice injected with this combination died. When examined after death, these mice were shown to have live slick bacteria in their blood. Somehow, the rough bacteria had given birth to slick bacteria in the bodies of the mice. The property of a slick membrane had been transferred to the rough bacteria. Griffith and others surmised that some substance had been freed by the slick bacteria and absorbed by the rough bacteria. No one knew what the substance was, but the researchers called it the "transforming principle."

In the 1940s, Oswald Avery, a physician at the Rockefeller Institute (now Rockefeller University), and his colleagues, Colin McLeod and Maclyn McCarty, set out to learn what the transforming principle was. They first discovered that the disease-producing slick bacteria had a special, lethal chemical in their cell walls. After these bacteria had been killed to make the vaccine, the ability to make the chemical was transferred to the previously harmless rough bacteria. After many months of study, Avery and his students determined how this transfer was possible: the chemical was transported via a material, a nucleic acid known as deoxyribonucleic acid, or DNA. The disease-causing bacteria, when they died, fell apart, and material from inside them was dispersed in the fluid in which they lived. The harmless bacteria absorbed some of this dispersed DNA. When the harmless bacteria had done so, they began to produce the chemical that made them lethal. DNA had transformed the harmless variety into a pneumonia-producing type. Avery and his colleagues had shown that Griffith's transforming principle was DNA.

The Dynamic Trio

In the early 1940s, a team of three scientists began a long and successful partnership at Cold Spring Harbor. Max Delbrück, the leader of the trio, had left Germany in 1937 to escape Adolf Hitler and National Socialism (Nazism). Delbrück's first faculty position was in the physics department of Vanderbilt University in Tennessee. After several years, he accepted an appointment at the California Institute of Technology in Pasadena. After 1947, he spent the school year in California and the summer months at Cold Spring Harbor.

The second team member was Salvador Luria. He had come to the United States in 1939, a refugee from Italy under Benito Mussolini's Fascist dictatorship. Luria was a professor at Indiana University in Bloomington. The third member was Alfred Hershey, a microbiologist who had received his Ph.D. from Michigan State University. In the early 1940s, Hershey was a member of the biology faculty at Vanderbilt University.

Delbrück, a physicist, and Luria, a physician and self-taught chemist, became colleagues at Cold Spring Harbor in the summer of 1940. Hershey, a microbiologist, started working with them during the summer of 1943. In 1950, Hershey accepted a research position at Cold Spring Harbor and remained a full-time resident scientist until he retired in 1970. The previous year, 1969, Delbrück, Luria, and Hershey were awarded the Nobel Prize for physiology.

Delbrück's desire to make biology into an experimental science began in 1933 while a student in Germany. Delbrück wanted to find orderly principles in biology like those that had been found in physics, so he sought out creatures that he thought might have the most orderly existence. The young scientist came to believe that microscopic bacteria, one of the simplest life forms, would be an excellent research subject. The single-celled organisms do not have a nucleus and exhibit a simplicity of function not seen in advanced creatures. That is, bacteria absorb nutrition from their immediate environment and grow and reproduce without much, if any, movement or other forms of behavior. After more study, Delbrück conceded that viruses might be even better for his research. A miniscule, uncomplicated virus does not ingest nourishment or eliminate waste. Indeed, at that time, some scientists questioned whether the virus was a living organism.

While studying these tiny creatures, Delbrück and his coworkers found that some viruses lived on or in bacteria. Because of this association, they were able to study the life cycles and interactions of these simple organisms. They discovered that the life cycle of a virus was often completed in less than 30 minutes. The Delbrück group determined to uncover what happened during the viruses' few minutes of life.

Luria, with the help of the improved electron microscope, saw that one variety of virus—a bacteriophage, or phage for short—had a round body and a slender tail. Hershey observed that the round-bodied viruses attached themselves to the surface of bacteria but did not enter the cell. He discovered that these viruses punctured the cell wall with their tails and injected their DNA into the body of the bacterium. The viruses' empty bodies then floated away from the infected bacterial cells. The scientists called these empty, floating bodies "ghosts."

Meanwhile, the injected molecules of nucleic acid use the raw materials and protein-manufacturing apparatus of the infected bacterial cell to duplicate themselves and to manufacture a skinlike covering of protein. The bacterial cell becomes filled with new viruses. Finally, the new viruses secrete an enzyme that dissolves the host bacteria. The

Max Delbrück was trained as a physicist but did outstanding experimental work in microbiology. (Courtesy of the National Library of Medicine)

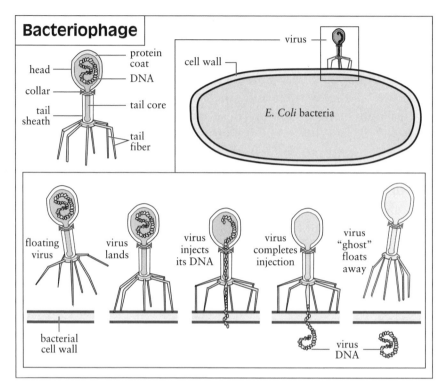

This representation of a virus attacking a bacterium is based on a sequence of images obtained from an electron microscope.

viruses are released to seek out and infect other bacteria. Seven years of painstaking research was needed to discover the complete story of these viruses.

In 1952, Hershey proved the point by a simple experiment. He and his coworker, Martha Chase, fed a colony of bacteria on nutrients to which some radioactive phosphorus and some radioactive sulfur were added. The idea behind the experiment was to take advantage of the fact that phosphorus is used in making nucleic acids and sulfur is not. Likewise, sulfur is used by viruses to make proteins but phosphorus is not. Hershey and Chase thought they could show that viruses took both phosphorus and sulfur from the bacteria they invaded but that when the viruses attacked fresh bacteria, only the radioactive phosphorus would be found inside such bacteria.

Hershey and Chase put live viruses into the colony of bacteria that had consumed radioactive nutrients. The infection and disintegration of the bacteria took about 20 minutes. The viruses had taken up some of the radioactive sulfur into their protein coats and had taken up the radioactive phosphorus into their DNA. These viruses had disintegrated all the bacteria from the first colony. Now Hershey and Chase used the new young viruses to infect another colony of bacteria that had not been fed radioactive material. They allowed the phages only about two minutes to find and infect new hosts. They then poured the material containing the viruses and the bacteria into an electric blender and turned on the motor. The rapidly whirling blades separated the bacteria from the viruses. The liquid was then spun in a centrifuge, a machine that separates materials by weight. The bacterial bodies weighing more than the viruses accumulated at the bottom of the centrifuge container. These bacterial bodies were rich in radioactive phosphorus but had no radioactive sulfur in them. The only source of radioactive phosphorus was the nucleic acid carried by the viruses. This meant that the invasion by the viruses was accomplished by the injection of nucleic acid. This proved that all the information needed to produce new viruses was

Alfred Hershey proved that the material injected by the virus into the bacterium was DNA. (Courtesy of the National Library of Medicine)

Salvador Luria was the first person to see the effects of a virus attack on a bacterium. (Courtesy of the National Library of Medicine)

carried by the injected nucleic acid.

James Watson, whose dissertation research was directed by Luria, was greatly influenced by Delbrück's group. In 1948, Watson spent the summer at Cold Spring Harbor, and Delbrück familiarized Watson with the ongoing virus research. Watson did not return to Cold Spring Harbor until the summer of 1953. By that time, he and his colleague Francis Crick had discovered the structure of DNA. Watson joined the faculty at Harvard University, and 15 years later, in 1968, became the part-time director of the Cold Spring Harbor Laboratory.

7
The Race for Glory

James Watson was a child prodigy and graduated from college at age 19. Three years later, he received his Ph.D. from Indiana University under Luria's supervision.

As a young man, Watson had little respect for other people's ideas. However, he did have great respect for Luria and Delbrück, and they, in turn, admired his ability. The older men arranged for the National Research Council to provide Watson with a postdoctoral grant in biochemistry.

Griffith, Avery and his coworkers, and others had established that nucleic acid was the key factor in inheritance. In the fall of 1950, Watson traveled to Denmark to study the chemistry of nucleic acid. It was still a mystery about how this chain of simple, slightly acidic sugarlike units could carry all the information needed to form a complete organism.

In the late spring of 1951, Watson and his Danish teachers went to a meeting in Naples, Italy. Watson attended a talk by Maurice Wilkins, a senior research scientist at King's College, London. Wilkins had developed a new method of using X-rays to study complicated biological molecules. With his technique, a sample of pure carbon-based molecules was solidified and then x-rayed. Wilkins discovered that a distinctive pattern of light and shadow then appeared on the photographic plate. The pattern was different for each type of molecule and correlated with its shape. For example, the image made by a coiled or spiral molecule is different from that made by a circular form. During earlier studies, Wilkins had obtained crude X-ray pictures of DNA but was unable to determine the details of structure. Nevertheless, he hoped that his new technique would show the main structure of complicated carbon-based substances, such as nucleic acid.

Maurice Wilkins's report inspired Watson to verify his chemical analysis of nucleic acid with the use of X-rays. He wrote to Delbrück and Luria and requested their assistance in obtaining work space at the Cavendish Laboratory at Cambridge University in England. The Cavendish Laboratory was a major research center in physics, and the staff there knew a great deal about X-rays. In fact, Francis Crick, an overage graduate student, was specifically interested in X-ray studies of biological molecules.

During his years as a graduate student, Crick had had some unfortunate experiences. The records of his graduate level research had been destroyed by a German bomb during World War II in 1940. He was therefore unable to write the dissertation necessary to gain a Ph.D. After this mishap, he had been recruited into military research by the British government. By 1951, when Watson arrived at Cambridge, Crick was trying to design a new dissertation project.

The two men were asked to share an office. They became friends. The brash young American and the brilliant but disorganized Englishman liked each other. Crick taught Watson about X-rays, and Watson taught Crick about viruses. They soon agreed on a common goal. They would be the first to determine the structure of DNA.

In Search of the Structure

Watson and Crick were well aware that their goal would be difficult to attain. They began their work by searching the scientific literature for reports on earlier DNA studies. These writings would allow them to assemble all the known facts and ideas on their chosen topic.

They quickly discovered that the scientific journals had not published a single, high-quality X-ray picture of DNA. Crick believed that good X-rays were essential to their research. Although he could photograph and interpret the pictures, Crick did not have any X-ray equipment of his own; therefore, he needed to analyze photographs that had been taken by other biochemists.

Watson and Crick asked Wilkins if they could study his X-rays of DNA. Wilkins was agreeable. However, the work being done at King's College had been assigned to Wilkins's colleague, Rosalind Franklin. Although Wilkins's previous X-ray pictures were cloudy, the images suggested that the DNA molecule was a double strand of twisted material. That twisted double strand is now called a double helix. The word *helix* is from the Greek work for spiral.

Wilkins and Franklin had always had a difficult working relationship. Wilkins thought that Franklin had been hired as his assistant. Franklin thought she had been given the job as an independent research scientist. By 1951, relations were strained, although they did cooperate on some activities. In November of that year, Wilkins organized a meeting in London to publicize Franklin's work. Watson attended the meeting.

When Watson returned to Cambridge, he and Crick discussed Franklin's ideas on DNA and the information that they had assembled. Franklin had said she was sure that her X-ray images indicated a double helix structure: two parallel strands, or "backbones," wound about each other with a fixed length for each turn in the helix. The other information available to Watson and Crick was the amount of each chemical element in a DNA molecule. They knew the precise proportions of each such chemical element: carbon, oxygen, nitrogen, hydrogen, and phosphorus.

They also knew how the crucial submolecules were formed and their respective shapes; that is, they knew the structure of deoxyribose, the slightly acidic sugarlike submolecule that was the most numerous of the submolecules. They also knew the structure, atom by atom, of the slightly alkaline (or basic) submolecules: cytosine, guanine, thymine, and adenine. (These molecules are called "bases.") Finally, they knew that the relative proportions among these bases was approximately equal and that their total quantity was equal to the number of sugarlike submolecules.

Two of the four alkaline submolecules, cytosine and thymine, are formed of a single ring of six atoms. The other two, adenine and guanine, are in the form of two connected rings—one of six atoms and one ring of five. Although all these rings are composed of nitrogen and carbon atoms, the positioning of the atoms is slightly different in each of the four submolecules. Using these facts, Watson and Crick designed and built a large-scale wire model of a DNA molecule. Small balls represented each element and short wires represented the bonds between the elements.

James Watson, the codiscoverer, with Francis Crick, of the structure of DNA (Courtesy of the National Library of Medicine)

The two men took the model to London and invited Wilkins, Franklin, and other scientists to look at it. The presentation was a total failure. All the experts agreed the model was inaccurate because some of the basic principles of physics and chemistry had been ignored. Watson and

Crick were embarrassed. They began work on new projects that were unrelated to the study of DNA.

Watson and Crick investigated other lines of research for about two years, but they continued to read and discuss new information on the structure of DNA. In January 1953, a report written by the Nobel Prize winner Linus Pauling revived their enthusiasm for DNA research. Pauling, one of the most respected biochemists in the world, proposed a model of a DNA molecule that had a three-stranded coil. Because Crick and Watson had seen Wilkins's X-rays, which seemed to indicate that DNA

Francis Crick examining the structural model of DNA (Courtesy of the National Archives Research Service)

was a two-stranded coil, they immediately recognized that Pauling's structure was probably incorrect. Pauling's apparent mistake actually inspired Watson and Crick to resume their own work on DNA.

The next month, Watson traveled to London to discuss the Pauling model with Wilkins and Franklin. The meeting was not fruitful. After the meeting, Wilkins invited Watson to his office and produced a copy of Franklin's clearest X-ray picture of DNA. This picture strongly reinforced their assumption that the basic structure of DNA was a two-stranded coil. After Watson returned to Cambridge, he and Crick built several large-scale models of DNA based on the double helix idea.

Crick and Watson reasoned that one base must be attached to each of the acidic, sugarlike submolecules that form the

Linus Pauling was a major figure in the field of biochemistry. He sought to find the structure of DNA but did not know that Watson and Crick were on the same quest. (Courtesy of the National Library of Medicine)

coiled backbones. They constructed a model showing the submolecules sticking out from the backbones. The two scientists soon decided that this arrangement was neither structurally nor chemically sound.

For the next model, Watson tried mounting the bases on the interior sides of the long, coiled backbones. He paired the one-ringed submolecule thymine with its one-ringed counterpart cytosine and the two-ringed submolecule of adenine with its two-ringed counterpart guanine. This arrangement, too, was incorrect. The pairing of one-ring particles alternating with the pairing of the bulkier two-ring particles resulted in an impossibly uneven and unstable structure.

On Saturday morning, February 21, 1953, Watson brought some pieces of cardboard to his office and placed them on the desk. He had made cutouts of the four alkaline submolecules and the sugarlike parts of the backbones. For a while, Watson arranged the pieces into various configurations. Suddenly, the light dawned. He saw the DNA molecule as a long spiral ladder. The backbones were the exterior supports, and the alkaline submolecules formed the rungs between the supports. The rungs would be even in size if a smaller, one-ringed submolecule and a larger, two-ringed submolecule always shared a rung.

Details of the Chemical Arrangement of DNA

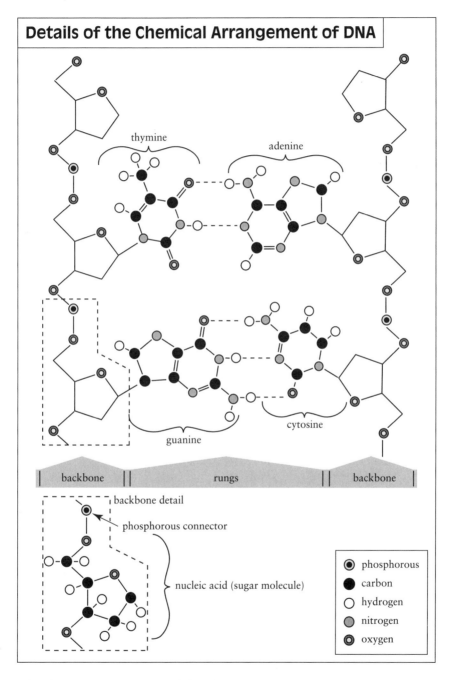

This drawing shows some of the chemical details in the structure of a short segment of DNA.

Watson realized that he must consider both the structural stability and the chemical requirements of the DNA molecule. In order to achieve the necessary chemical connections, the submolecule of thymine must always be paired with that of adenine and the submolecule of cytosine with that of guanine. Watson carefully constructed the model of DNA in accord with his new ideas. The structure was then examined by Crick and later, by Wilkins and Franklin. All approved of this model of DNA.

Watson and Crick introduced the model in March 1953. The report was published in *Nature*, an important science journal. The same issue included articles written by Wilkins and Franklin in support of the theory. Nine years later, in 1962, Watson, Crick, and Wilkins shared the Nobel Prize in physiology or medicine for their work. Unfortunately, Rosalind Franklin had died in 1958. Most biochemists and geneticists believe that Franklin's work was vital to the scientific breakthrough and that she should have shared in the honors. However, rules governing Nobel prizes state that only living people may receive the awards.

Completing the Analysis

In 1953, as soon as the DNA model was accepted, Watson and Crick began work to confirm their theory. They believed that the complicated but logical structure was strong and satisfied both the biological and chemical requirements of a stable molecule.

Indeed, as a carrier of genetic blueprints, their proposed structure seemed to meet three essential conditions. In order to convey genetic information from generation to generation, the DNA molecule had to be resilient and sturdy. The positioning of the bases on the protected inward side of the spiral ladder accomplished that condition. The molecule also had to make exact duplicates of itself. The research of many scientists determined that the proposed structure of the DNA molecule allowed this duplication. Lastly, the DNA molecule had to carry the large amount of information needed to make a living creature. Future analyses proved that the arrangement of the bases on the spiral strands permitted this outcome. In 1953, leading biochemists and molecular biologists agreed that the model possessed the necessary characteristics. And they still agree.

This agreement is largely based on a single fact. In the model, a sequence of bases occupies each strand of the double-stranded molecule. The bases on one strand are arranged to complement the bases on the other strand; in other words, each base is linked with its chemical complement. The structure of the model reveals that adenine and thymine are always linked on the same rung. In the same manner, guanine is the complement of cytosine.

The first letter of each submolecule is used in the shorthand of genetics notation. *A* stands for adenine, *G* for guanine, *T* for thymine, and *C* for cytosine. According to the shorthand, *A* always pairs with its chemical complement *T*, and *G* with *C*. If the series of bases on one strand is A T T G C C A C A C, then the series on the second strand *must be* T A A C G G T G T G.

When cell division occurs, two identical cells are formed. Each new cell must carry all the genetic information of the parent cell. The original DNA, therefore, must be copied. To do this, the DNA molecule splits down its length. This can be compared to unzipping a zipper. When the strands—or the two parts of the zipper—pull apart, the process of duplication begins. With the help of several special enzymes, a new strand forms on each old strand. The new strand will be an exact complement of the old strand. An old strand that reads A T T G C C A C A will get a new partner with the T A A C G G T G T pattern and vice versa. After this operation, there are two identical spirals, one for the old cell and one for the new cell.

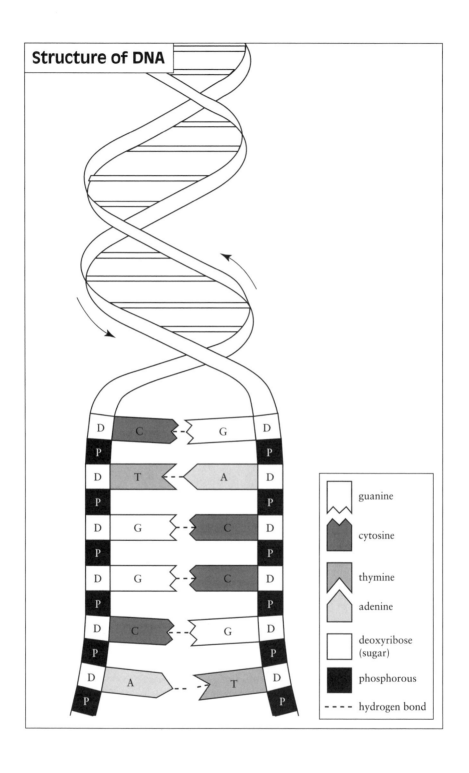

Structure of DNA

guanine

cytosine

thymine

adenine

deoxyribose (sugar)

phosphorous

- - - - hydrogen bond

To help ensure that each strand of DNA has been correctly manufactured, cells have established a sort of quality control. For a few seconds, the new strand and the old strand share the same cell. In this brief span of time, the arrangement of bases on the newly manufactured strand is checked for accuracy. If a mistake has been made, the enzymes correct the faulty sequence based on the information contained in the old strand.

Other Outcomes

After publishing their revolutionary report, Crick remained at Cambridge. For several years, Watson taught biochemistry at Harvard University and worked as a part-time researcher at the Cold Spring Harbor Laboratory. In 1977, Watson assumed the full-time directorship of the Cold Spring Harbor Laboratory. He held that position when Barbara McClintock received her Nobel Prize in 1983.

opposite page: A schematic representation of a short stretch of a DNA molecule. Each DNA molecule is made up of two "backbones" composed of alternating units of phosphorous (P) and deoxyribose (D), a sugar. The backbones have the shape of a helix or coil, and they twine around each other. Inside the backbones, like rungs on a ladder, are four submolecules called bases. The bases always connect to a particular partner base by a hydrogen bond. Adenine (A) always pairs with thymine (T), and cytosine (C) always pairs with guanine (G).

8

The Code

James Watson and Francis Crick were not geneticists. They thought of themselves as biochemists or molecular biologists. However, their ability to visualize the physical and chemical structure of DNA was recognized by scientists in all fields. Indeed, geneticists and other specialists were readily convinced that the genes of all creatures are composed of DNA. They accepted the fact that DNA carries information about biological traits, such as eye color. However, the processes that allow the transmission of these inherited traits were still not understood. If genes convey information, something in the cells of living creatures must be able to decode and use that information. There must be a language of the genes. Attempts to learn how the body's cells convey genetic information were begun long before either Watson or Crick was born.

How the Genes Work

When Gregor Mendel's rediscovered work was publicized by de Vries and other scientists in 1900, Walter Sutton, an American biologist, became interested in testing the Mendelian theory. In 1902, he began to investigate the actions of chromosomes during cell division. Using a microscope, he saw that chromosomes made exact duplicates of themselves prior to the actual separation of the cells. Based on that observation,

Sutton reasoned correctly that chromosomes are the carriers of inherited traits. He published his theory in 1903.

A few years later, interest in Mendelian laws led to the founding of a new branch of science called "population genetics." This science concerns the laws of inheritance and how inherited characteristics can be traced in families, segments of the population, and entire communities of both humans and nonhuman species.

Biologists concerned with population genetics began to study human families with members who suffered from the same disease. They believed that such diseases might be inherited and that this work might shed light on Mendel's laws of inherited traits. Archibald Garrod was a British physician involved in part-time genetic research. He was impressed by the frequency with which a unique form of arthritis appeared in the members of an extended family group. In the early 1900s, Garrod began to study the medical histories of 48 members of one family. He found that for every two individuals suffering from arthritis, three were free from the disease. Even though the mathematical match was not perfect, Garrod saw a similarity between his findings and Mendel's observations on the laws of inheritance in sweet peas. Mendel's law states that a recessive trait (such as that of arthritis) appears in one out of four instances in a family group. Garrod was confident that the laws of inheritance for sweet peas also governed inheritance in humans. The physician published these conclusions in 1909.

As Garrod further analyzed the medical histories of those people with arthritis, he reasoned that the disease was caused by the blockage of a basic biological function. He further speculated that the blockage was due to the failure of a single enzyme. Enzymes are molecules that promote biochemical reactions in the body. Garrod also believed that other diseases might result from faulty enzymes and that such faulty enzymes might be the result of a mutation. Although no one understands how he arrived at these conclusions, his speculations are now known to be correct. Sadly, Garrod's work was unappreciated by his peers. His findings were at least 20 years ahead of their time.

Between 1910 and the late 1930s, the most important projects in genetic research were carried out by Thomas Hunt Morgan and his many students. At first, Morgan did not believe the theories of either Sutton or Garrod. However, Morgan had an open mind. When his research supported Sutton's ideas, he changed his position. He argued that genes reside in chromosomes and that changes in inherited traits are caused by mutations of the genes.

Amino Acids and Proteins

Other lines of research in biochemistry contributed to the eventual understanding of the role of DNA. Indeed, scientists had used biochemical methods long before Watson and Crick determined that genes are composed of DNA. As early as 1802, biochemists in the Netherlands began to analyze the structure of proteins. They discovered that protein molecules are assembled from small submolecules now called "amino acids." The Dutch scientists theorized that a prescribed assembly of amino acids forms a specific protein.

In 1806, the first amino acid was isolated and identified. By this time, scientists knew that there were thousands of different kinds of proteins. Eventually, 20 amino acids were identified as the building blocks of the thousands of proteins in living organisms.

George Beadle and Edward Tatum were among the first scientists to show how DNA and genes were linked to the amino acids and proteins. Beadle had studied under Morgan at the California Institute of Technology and then had joined Barbara McClintock's team of graduate students at Cornell.

Tatum was a biochemist who had studied at the University of Chicago and in Europe. They began a collaboration in 1937 at Stanford University. They were convinced that genes control enzymes and that enzymes control the workings of cells. In 1941, even before the structure of DNA was known, their research produced a major advance toward deciphering the genetic code.

Their studies began with an attempt to understand the forces that control the eye color of fruit flies. By analyzing the huge chromosomes of the flies' salivary glands, Beadle and Tatum identified the enzyme that helps control eye color. They also recognized how a mutant gene could disrupt this control. Although the work was successful, the studies progressed slowly.

In order to speed up their work, they began to use common bread molds rather than fruit flies as their research subjects. The bread mold cells grew rapidly in test colonies and fed on sugar and a few minerals. Beadle and Tatum used X-rays to produce mold-cell mutations. They hoped the X-rays would change the mold's ability to manufacture essential nutrients. After many failed attempts, they achieved a mutant bread mold that could not manufacture vitamin B_6. Although normal mold produces this essential vitamin, the mutant cells required a vitamin B_6 supplement to stay alive.

George Beadle and his coworkers proved that genes hold the recipes for the construction of proteins. (Courtesy of the National Library of Medicine)

Beadle and Tatum had succeeded in destroying the mold's ability to manufacture an essential vitamin.

Beadle and Tatum then set out to investigate a much more complicated subject. They hoped to disrupt the genes that normally produce amino acid molecules. They once again exposed bread mold to X-rays. Soon, tests showed that some of the mold cells required supplements of amino acids to remain alive. The cells now lacked the ability to produce a particular amino acid. This outcome confirmed that X-rays could damage the genes that govern amino acid production and disrupt the manufacture of proteins.

To identify which of the 20 amino acids was no longer being manufactured, Beadle and Tatum designed another series of tests. They placed small amounts of the affected mold, sugar, mineral salts, and water in each of 20 containers. In addition, each container received a drop containing molecules of one amino acid. When one of the bread mold samples was restored to health, Beadle and Tatum identified which amino acid had been missing. Genes are responsible for the manufacture of all amino acids; therefore, the fact that one amino acid was missing meant that the X-rays had caused a specific gene to stop making a specific amino acid. The two scientists completed their experiments by interfering with and then replacing many different amino acids. Their research demonstrated the link between genes and their control of amino acids.

The Basic Rules of Genetics

In 1957, four years after completing his work with Watson, Crick developed a new theory based in part on the research done by Beadle and Tatum. He was also aided by American physicist George Gamow, who believed that DNA carries the information necessary to assemble amino acids into protein chains. Gamow approached the problem of the DNA code as if it were a mathematical puzzle and put forward a series of possible solutions.

Crick knew that DNA molecules are chains as are protein molecules, and he wondered whether the similar structures might indicate a further correlation between proteins and DNA. He reasoned that the arrangement of submolecules, or bases, on the DNA chain might correspond to the arrangement of amino acids on the protein chain. If this was the case, a segment of DNA would be the gene that carries the information to construct a specific protein.

Crick further theorized that the arrangement of amino acids on a protein chain defines both the composition and the function of protein molecules. For example, a protein chain might consist of 100, 200, or more than 500 submolecules, or amino acids. The composition of the chain might be two submolecules of one type of amino acid, three of another type, five of the third, two of the fourth, and on and on. The exact arrangement and number of amino acids in the protein chain is designated by the exact arrangement and number of submolecules in each gene. The sequence of amino acids determines whether the protein serves as a building block of the cell or as an enzyme to speed the inner workings of the cell. Crick wrote an article about the theory. By correlating the genetic code of DNA to the code of the protein chain, Crick had identified the basic process of inheritance.

The Wording of the Code

Crick and his fellow workers also developed a concept that explained how they believed the DNA code was arranged into messages that were understandable to the cell. According to their theory, in order to build the required protein molecule, a combination of bases in the DNA chain must be programmed to connect with one of the 20 amino acids. After careful chemical analysis, the scientists determined that any three of the four bases in DNA (A, T, G, and C) must be present to call the needed amino acid. A set of three bases (such as TAT or TTT) was called a "codon," from the word *code*.

Crick's team believed that each codon is able to summon a specific amino acid. The three bases can be assembled into 64 different combinations, or codons. Since there are 64 codons and only 20 different amino acids, it seemed likely that some amino acids could be summoned by more than one codon. This idea has been proved correct. Further research has demonstrated that certain codons not only command protein construction but also signal the beginning and end of a gene.

While much of Crick's team's theory has proved correct, additional elements were later uncovered. One of these elements was the role of ribonucleic acid, or RNA. RNA is like DNA except that it has a different kind of sugar—ribose—in its backbone, and in place of thymine, it has the base uracil. DNA cannot usually leave the cell nucleus, but some types of RNA can travel into the areas of the cell where proteins are constructed.

Marshall Nirenberg did the laboratory work that supported Francis Crick's idea that a set of three bases in the DNA chain determines which amino acid will be entered in the peptide sequence. (Courtesy of the National Library of Medicine)

In the 1960s, Marshall Warren Nirenberg, a genetic researcher at the National Institutes of Health in Bethesda, Maryland, hoped to test the theory developed by Crick and Gamow that codons summon specific amino acids. By 1961, he devised a method to produce a strand of RNA (which is usually singular in form, as opposed to the double strands found in a complete molecule of DNA). He used only one base— U (uracil)—to compose the strand. Nirenberg's nucleic acid strand read UUU, UUU, UUU, UUU, and so on. He placed a sample of the UUU strands and a drop of one of the amino acids in each of 20 flasks. Chemical tests showed that only one of the amino acids, phenylalanine, linked to the UUU strands of nucleic acid. This result strongly supported the idea that each combination of three bases specifies one particular amino acid.

Har Gobind Khorana extended Nirenberg's finding by showing how the different combinations of three bases were each linked to a particular amino acid. (Courtesy of the National Library of Medicine)

Other scientists, such as Har Gobind Khorana, soon followed Nirenberg's example and produced samples of other segments of RNA constructed from a single type of base molecule codon such as CCC. Khorana verified that each such codon links to a particular amino acid. More advanced techniques allowed the production of mixed combinations of three bases. Each codon of this type, such as CAG, linked to one and only one amino acid.

The genetic code had been broken. Scientists could now say that each codon in the set of 64 combinations coded for a specific amino acid. Each triplet on a DNA strand, such as

GTT, AGG, or CTA, translated through RNA, called for a different amino acid. Scientists realized that codons directed the production of the proteins.

After the code had been broken, scientists understood why codons are positioned in a specific order on the long spiral strand of DNA. It seemed likely that a specific arrangement of these codons corresponded to the arrangement of amino acids in a protein; therefore, the sequence of amino acids mirrored the sequence of codons in the gene.

The Cell as a Production Plant

The human body is an assembly of vast numbers of cells. Indeed, all nonmicroscopic plants and animals contain hundreds, hundreds of thousands, or even billions of cells. Inside each of these cells is a small structure called a nucleus. Within the nucleus are still smaller particles. These particles of matter contain almost all the cell's genetic material. At most times during the cell's life, a strand of DNA—the carrier of this genetic information—looks like a long piece of roughly woven string. The parts of this structure are difficult to distinguish under even the most powerful electron microscope.

Even though this activity cannot be seen, chemical analyses prove that the double strands of DNA uncouple along their full length when a cell is ready to divide. Enzymes go to work, and each of the single strands is provided with a new partner called a complement. In all body cells except sex cells, when this duplication process is completed, there are twice the original number of double helices. Each double helix folds up and is compressed into a chromosome. The chromosomes then move to opposite sides of the cell and the cell splits down the middle. Each new cell has the same DNA information as the parent cell. When cell division is complete, the DNA that has been packed into the chromosomes is unpacked. The DNA

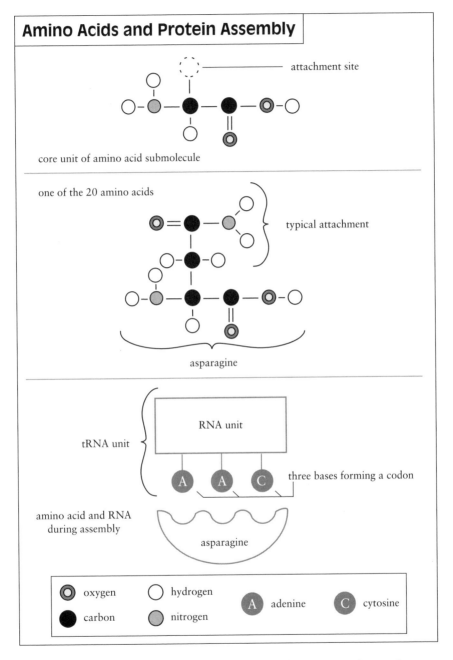

Amino Acids and Protein Assembly

attachment site

core unit of amino acid submolecule

one of the 20 amino acids

typical attachment

asparagine

tRNA unit

RNA unit

three bases forming a codon

amino acid and RNA during assembly

asparagine

oxygen   hydrogen   adenine   cytosine
carbon   nitrogen

All the amino acid submolecules can be attached to one another to form a chain. The front end of one fits neatly into the back end of the preceding submolecule.

resumes the shape of long pieces of string. The cell now begins work on the production of proteins.

Under a strong microscope, scientists can observe several dozen distinctive structures within a typical cell. Some act to transport nutrients throughout the cell, and others rid the cell of waste materials. Although all contribute to the life of the cell, the most important structures are the ribosomes. The ribosomes serve the cell by manufacturing proteins. They construct both the protein molecules used for building blocks and the protein molecules used as enzymes. The enzymes promote the chemical reactions that regulate the activities of the cell.

In order to build a particular protein, a double strand of DNA opens enough to expose a specific sequence of bases. This sequence is the gene that holds the protein recipe. The unzipping necessary to produce a protein is similar to the unzipping that takes place before cell division. However, the amount of DNA needed to build one protein may be only a few hundred to a few thousand bases in length. Prior to cell division, hundreds of millions of bases must be duplicated.

When the required gene is exposed, RNA forms a complementary copy of the gene. Although the structure of an RNA molecule is very similar to that of DNA, RNA is far shorter than DNA and is not in the form of a double helix. Indeed, RNA is a single untwisted strand that equals the length of a gene.

The relatively short, single uncoiled strand of RNA is now the complement of the base sequence contained in the unzipped gene. The RNA strand uncouples from the gene and moves out of the nucleus. This kind of RNA molecule is called messenger RNA, or mRNA, because it carries the gene's coded message into the body of the cell.

Once outside the nucleus, the mRNA molecule makes a complementary copy of itself. Then the mRNA is no longer needed and is recycled by the enzymes present in the cell. The newest copy of the protein recipe is called ribosomal RNA, or rRNA, because it attaches itself to the ribosome. The rRNA

Protein Synthesis

amino acids

new protein

ribosome

AUA CCA AAA CCC AUC GCU UGG GUG UGU UCU AGU GGA CCA AUU CCC GGU UGG

alanine

see detail

tRNA

aspartic acid

G A U

serine

A G C

amino acids

valine

serine

A G U

alanine

G C U

sets of three bases (codons)

mRNA molecule

DETAIL

amino acid

tRNA

G C U

C C C A U C U G G

part of the mRNA molecule

Molecules of transfer RNA bring amino acids into line, linking them together to form a protein that follows the plan carried by the messenger RNA.

controls the actual production of protein molecules; therefore, the ribosome uses the instructions on the rRNA to produce the required protein.

Another form of RNA is always present in the main body of the cell. These pieces of RNA are relatively short and contain the codon, or triple set of bases, that can link to a particular amino acid. These RNA molecules are responsible for capturing the required amino acids that float freely in the main body of the cell. This form of RNA is known as transfer RNA, or tRNA, because it catches and transports the amino acids to the ribosome-manufacturing centers in the cell.

The protein recipe on the rRNA determines the type and arrangement of amino acids required to build the protein. The amino acid molecules are summoned in the prescribed order and attached, one by one, in a string. This specific sequence of amino acids defines the type of protein and its function. In 25 to 35 seconds, a ribosome can produce a protein chain of 300 to 500 amino acids.

The rapid production of proteins proceeds in many ribosomes at the same time. Since several ribosomes can produce the same type of protein at the same time, a given protein molecule can be manufactured every three seconds. If the cell has 300,000 rRNA molecules working at one time, it can therefore produce 100,000 proteins per second.

There is much to learn about the activities that take place within the cell. For example, when protein production begins, the DNA strands uncouple. Each strand is exposed and could be copied onto mRNA; however, it seems that one strand is copied and the other is not. Theory suggests that this is one of the safeguards used to protect heredity. Since the uncopied strand is not acted upon by enzymes to make the mRNA complement, it is less likely to be damaged. Therefore, the integrity of the uncopied strand is safeguarded and can be used as backup for the future duplication.

Accidents can happen to the genetic material carried by the cell. By mistake, the material can be incorrectly transported within and between chromosomes. In addition, DNA from another cell can enter the cell and become a part of a gene. However, the risk of a lethal modification in the gene structure is slight because the primary genetic information is carefully guarded by the double-strand arrangement.

9

Genetic Analysis

Har Gobind Khorana and others were able to analyze short segments of nucleic acid and even to construct synthetic strands of tRNA. However, no one had yet mapped the full sequence of base pairs in a gene.

Each human cell contains about 30,000 genes. Each of these genes contains the plan for a particular protein. Most genes in most cells, however, are inactive, or dormant. These genes are not engaged in any form of work; in the language of genetics, they are unexpressed. Indeed, in a brain cell, for example, only genes predetermined to support that particular type of cell are active, or expressed. In a muscle cell, a different set of genes is at work. "Housekeeping" genes, however, are active at all times in all cells. These genes make the proteins that build the walls and interior structures that are necessary to every cell.

In addition to large numbers of unexpressed genes, each cell contains DNA that is always inactive. These segments of DNA contribute nothing to the genes and, indeed, are not part of true genes. Some geneticists characterize this material as "junk DNA." Others are more cautious and believe that its purpose is not yet understood.

Some of this inactive DNA occurs within the sequences that make up true genes. When a gene is being transcribed onto messenger RNA (mRNA), the junk segments are transcribed along with the segments of genetic information. Once incorporated in the mRNA, special enzymes force these nonfunctional scraps into loops. The loops are pushed aside and cut out by the enzymes. No one completely understands how the enzymes can distinguish true RNA from junk RNA.

In addition to the inactive DNA within a gene, there is inactive DNA between genes. A strand of DNA might include a typical gene of 3,000 base pairs followed by 10,000 base pairs of junk DNA and then another true gene of 4,000 base pairs. A similar sequence of junk DNA and true genes will continue along the entire length of the strand. The length of each segment of junk DNA can vary from a few hundred to several thousand base pairs. The lengths of the junk DNA segments found within and between true genes differ from person to person.

Separating Large Molecules

In 1906, a Russian botanist, Mikhail Tsvett, wanted to separate and analyze the chemical compounds that give flowers their color. He speculated that the various pigments were molecules of different sizes. Tsvett made a solution of crushed flowers and alcohol and dripped the solution into a tube containing powdered metal salts. He reasoned that the largest molecules would remain near the top, the smallest would filter to the bottom, and the others would be separated according to their size. The separation process worked as Tsvett had hoped. He then analyzed the separated molecules to find their chemical composition.

This technique is known as chromatography. Its name comes from *chromo,* the Greek word for "color," since it was first used to separate pigment molecules. However, chromatography is now used to separate mixtures of large, carbon-based molecules. In 1915, Richard Willstatter won the Nobel Prize in chemistry for inventing a technique similar to chromatography. His method was used to separate the different varieties of chlorophyll molecules, the pigments that absorb light energy and allow green plants to manufacture sugars from carbon dioxide and water.

Over the years, scientists have developed other variations of chromatography. At present, materials such as small beads of resin, gels (clear gelatin), and paper are used to separate large carbon-based molecules. For example, paper chromatography provides a quick way to analyze a mixture of water-soluble molecules. Samples of a mixture such as ink are placed almost an inch (2 cm) from the bottom edge of a piece of white blotting paper. The piece of paper is hung above a pan of water with about a half-inch (1 cm) of the bottom edge submerged in the water. The water and ink rise through the blotting paper. The largest and heaviest molecules of ink will rise the shortest distance up the paper while the smallest and lightest molecules will rise the farthest distance upward.

In the 1920s, refinements in the technique of chromatography were developed by several chemists. The Swedish scientist Arne Wilhelm Kaurin Tiselius invented a process known as electrophoresis, which separated carbon-based molecules by electrical attraction and size. Tiselius's method was similar to paper chromatography, but the paper used in his technique was laid flat on a ceramic plate. The paper was wetted with a solution of salt, and one edge was attached to a powerful electric current. Samples of carbon-based materials were deposited along the opposite edge of the paper. When the electric current was turned on, all the molecules in the mixture were attracted to the electrode. The smaller molecules moved farther than the larger molecules so that patches of different molecules formed on the sheet. When the electric current was switched off, the separate patches of carbon-based molecules could be clearly seen. The paper was cut into several sections to isolate the various assemblies of molecules according to their attraction to electricity and size. Each section was analyzed to determine the chemical composition of that assembly. Tiselius won the Nobel Prize in chemistry in 1948 for this work.

During the middle decades of the 1900s, several scientists won Nobel Prizes for their advanced applications of these techniques. One such prize winner was Frederick Sanger.

Sanger was born in a small English village in 1918. His father was a physician and the family was relatively prosperous. Sanger enrolled in Cambridge University in 1937. He remained at Cambridge for his graduate training and in 1943 received his doctoral degree in biochemistry. After his graduation, Sanger accepted a post as a research scientist at Cambridge and began studying the biochemistry of proteins.

In 1958, Sanger was awarded the Nobel Prize in chemistry for his use of chromatography in discovering the composition of insulin, the hormone that regulates the amount of sugar in the blood. (Sanger won another Nobel Prize in chemistry in 1980 for using the techniques of chromatography and electrophoresis to determine the composition of DNA segments.)

Protein Studies

By the early 1940s, most scientists were convinced that protein molecules such as insulin are assemblies of amino acid submolecules. Indeed, some believed that these submolecules are linked into chains. By this time, all 20 amino acids had been identified and analyzed. For a few specific proteins, the amino acids at the ends of the chain had been identified. However, little was known about the exact formation of a protein molecule or the specific location of the majority of amino acids that were part of it.

Insulin is an unusual protein. It is composed of two parallel strands of amino acids rather than one long strand. When Sanger began studying the exact structure of insulin, biochemists

Insulin Molecule

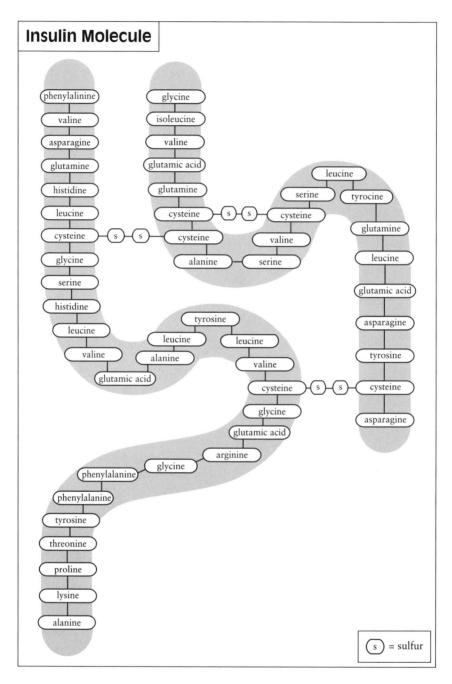

This diagram of an insulin molecule shows the sequence of amino acids and the two cross-links and the one self-link made by sulfur atoms.

thought that a single insulin molecule might be composed of as many as eight parallel strands. Later studies seemed to indicate four strands. Sanger proved that each insulin molecule contained two, relatively short, roughly parallel strands of amino acids.

Sanger's next studies located three pairs of sulfur atoms in each insulin molecule. Sulfur atoms were known to act as bridges between pairs of amino acids. Sanger reasoned that two of the pairs linked the two strands of amino acids. Later research found that the third pair of sulfur atoms linked one amino acid submolecule with another in the same strand. Several submolecules divided the linked amino acids and these formed a loop in the strand.

Sanger next established that the short strand of human insulin consists of 20 amino acids and the other of 30. The loop is always in the shorter strand. Sanger had determined the basic structure of an insulin molecule.

Sanger next sought to determine the composition of that structure. He hoped to define the specific amino acids and the quantity of each amino acid found on each strand of the insulin molecule. Through the use of special chemicals, he separated the chains of protein molecules. He separated the longer chain from the shorter by chromatography. He then worked on each chain by itself.

Frederick Sanger defined the sequence of amino acids in insulin and went on to sequence RNA and DNA. (Courtesy of the National Library of Medicine)

The next step was to break the chains into individual amino acids and begin a study of these submolecules. He made a solution of the amino acids from one of the chains and placed a large sample of it near the corner of a sheet of blotting paper. In this method of chromatography, the water carries the smallest and lightest of the amino acids toward the top of the sheet. The submolecules of amino acid were distributed according to size along the edge of the paper.

Sanger then used electrophoresis to continue his analysis. Using the same sheet of paper, he attached an electrode to the side opposite the path of the amino acids. The submolecules now reacted in accord with their attraction to the electric current. Those most attracted moved the farthest distance from the edge of the paper, and the least attracted moved the shortest distance. The amino acids were thereby divided by both size and electrical attraction. Each carefully divided assembly of submolecules contained one kind of amino acid. The assemblies were cut apart and the contents of each were dissolved separately. The amount of material was weighed and analyzed by techniques that broke down the amino acids into their separate atoms. In this way, each type of amino acid was identified, and the amount of each type was determined.

Sanger's research had uncovered the structure of the two chains that make up an insulin molecule. He had identified the types and quantities of the amino acids on those protein chains. He next sought to identify the order in which the amino acids appeared. Sanger found enzymes that could sever the insulin strands into fragments of varying lengths. After the cuts were made, there would be a jumble of fragments, but the fragments could be organized again by using chromatography. With chromatography, he could tell how large each fragment was and thus how many amino acids it contained. Using chemical techniques, he could identify the amino acids on the ends of each fragment. When he had looked at many fragments, he could see some overlapping segments, such as AxxxD and

AxxC, which suggested that the string might be AxxCD, the x's standing for unknown amino acids. By repeating the process many times, the sequential pattern of amino acids could be read—first for one string and then for the other. Finally, the whole picture of the insulin molecule could be seen. Sanger's work was the first instance of an exact identification of the order of amino acids in any protein molecule.

The method was soon adopted by others. Since the 1950s, biochemists have analyzed many proteins: scientists now know the exact composition of several thousand human proteins, but at least 60,000 more remain to be analyzed.

RNA Studies

By 1960, Sanger's methods of protein analysis were well established, and others were carrying on the work. Sanger next began to study the composition of RNA. Indeed, his research on proteins had set the stage for the analysis of RNA. Messenger RNA contains the code for a particular protein. By looking at the sequence of amino acids in a particular protein, a biochemist could deduce the sequence of codons needed to direct the production of that protein. In other words, one could work backward from the amino acid to the codon. The set of three bases in the codon could then be specified. The difficult technical problem that remained was isolating the specific codon in each case because some amino acids are specified by more than one codon. Consequently, the paper electrophoretic techniques had to be employed again to separate the strands of RNA into small chunks that could be analyzed atom by atom using standard chemical analysis methods.

Sanger chose to work on the arrangement of the codons in the mRNA molecule because there were some naturally short versions. Using strong chemicals, he could break up one strand into smaller pieces and do his overlap analysis on the very short segments. This approach worked well, and Sanger was soon able to go on to the greater challenge of analyzing DNA.

DNA Sequencing

Unfortunately, there are no short molecules of DNA. By 1960, all known molecules of DNA were hundreds of thousands of base pairs in length. Scientists used strong chemicals to sever these strands into fragments. The use of these chemicals to break up the strands brought some risk that the internal composition of the DNA would be damaged.

Then in the early 1960s, researchers made an interesting discovery. They found that some bacteria, such as *Escherichia coli (E. coli)*, were immune to certain viruses. Further study showed that these bacteria produced enzymes that cut the viral DNA into small pieces. These enzymes are called "restriction enzymes." Researchers observed that each cut was made at a particular sequence of base pairs.

The restriction enzymes produced by the bacteria protect the bacteria from infection by the virus. When the viral DNA is cut up, the pieces could no longer make new proteins, so the virus could no longer multiply inside the bacterium. The bacteria that possessed such enzymes were immune from viral attack.

Further research found that other bacteria produced similar enzymes. Each of the enzymes was programmed to sever the strand of DNA at a different group of base pairs. By using different enzymes to divide a strand of DNA, scientists could obtain samples of various lengths. Sanger used some of these enzymes to produce an array of pieces of DNA. As before, the bases at the beginning of the strand and at the end of the strand could be identified. Sanger could then follow the mix-and-match technique used to determine the protein and RNA sequences to define DNA sequences.

In 1980, Sanger received his second Nobel Prize in chemistry for determining long sequences of bases in DNA. Because of his research, scientists could begin the task of reading all the base pairs in all the DNA in human and nonhuman cells. However, Sanger's method of decoding required a week to read fragments of DNA containing a few hundred to a few thousand base pairs. Scientists know that 3 billion base pairs are included in a single human cell. The task of decoding all the genes in a human cell, the full genome, was going to be a long and difficult one.

DNA Profiling

By the late 1970s, many research scientists in the United States had begun to use Sanger's fragmentation tests to analyze genetic materials from a variety of organisms. Ray White, a biologist from the University of Massachusetts at Worcester, was studying the genetic makeup of insects. During a convention in the summer of 1978, White was approached by David Botstein. Botstein, a scientist from the Massachusetts Institute of Technology, told White of a project aimed at linking genetic diseases with patterns of DNA fragments. The project was based on the idea that a person destined to develop a genetic disease might show specific pattern of bases in his or her DNA. The research project was being planned by the faculty and research staff at the University of Utah and the Howard Hughes Medical Research Institute associated with the university's medical school.

White was interested in working on the project and joined the staff at the Hughes Institute that autumn. By 1979, he had completed a study using electrophoresis. His work resulted in several important discoveries. For example, White was the first scientist to confirm that DNA patterns are unique for each human individual. He had discovered a way to identify a person by the pattern made by chromatographic distribution of strands of his or her DNA.

DNA Analysis and Crime Detection

Since the early 1900s, police have methodically analyzed materials found at crime scenes. At first, scientific detective work tended to focus on medical issues relating to the crime. Autopsies were performed on victims of sudden or violent death to determine time of death, cause of death, and other circumstances such as the victim's last meal.

Gradually, the scope of scientific investigations expanded to include techniques such as the identification of paper used in a ransom note or fibers from a garment worn by a possible culprit. However, the use of science in criminal detection varied widely in different jurisdictions of the United States and among European countries. Most often, medical pathologists and consulting chemists, who were not police officials, were brought in to study cases on an irregular basis.

In the 1930s, such arrangements began to change. In 1934, the U.S. Department of Justice brought together a permanent staff of scientists and technicians in Washington, D.C. This staff formed the core of the forensic science unit of the Federal Bureau of Investigation (FBI). The FBI program became the model for city and state police organizations throughout the United States.

Blood typing was used as a means of identification before the advent of modern genetic technology. Just after 1900, Karl Landsteiner, a German biochemist, isolated and identified the factors that influence the clotting of blood. Police tested both victims and possible perpetrators to learn whether their blood types were A, B, AB, or O. The types are distinguished by the enzymes found on the surface of red blood cells.

As a means of identification, blood typing is of limited value. Between 45 to 50 percent of U.S. citizens have type O blood; therefore, if this type of blood is found at a crime scene, few suspects can be eliminated. If type B blood is found, however, the culprit might be easier to convict, because only 10 to 20 percent of U.S. citizens have this blood type.

Since the 1900s, the discovery of additional blood factors has aided in the process of identification. However, judges and juries involved in serious criminal cases are seldom influenced by this evidence. Most are aware that this form of identification could never be absolute.

The possibility of using DNA as a reliable factor in identification became apparent in the early 1980s. In 1980, near a small village in the English Midlands, a 15-year-old girl was raped and murdered while on her way home from school. Three years later, on the same country lane, a second rape and murder took place. Police arrested a person who worked at a nearby mental institution. The man confessed to the second murder but strongly denied any knowledge of the first. The police were certain that both murders had been committed by the same person and were skeptical of this confession. They soon turned to Alec Jeffreys, a well-regarded molecular biologist on the faculty at Leicester University. The police hoped that Jeffreys could gain information about the culprit or culprits from testing samples of body fluids found at the crime scene. They needed to know whether both crimes had been committed by the same person and whether they had that person under arrest.

Jeffreys processed the DNA samples with enzymes and used gel electrophoresis to gain a distinctive pattern of blots. His analysis proved that both crimes had been committed by the same assailant but that the police did not have the right man. The man who had made the false confession was promptly released. The police had lost their only suspect.

The investigators decided to utilize DNA identification to expand their search. They required all local men between the ages of 18 and 35 to provide a blood sample for DNA testing. More than 5,000 samples were collected. The forensic laboratory of Scotland Yard, Britain's metropolitan police force, conducted most of the analyses. While the mass testing was under way, the police were informed of an interesting conversation overheard at a local tavern. A young man had bragged about fooling the police. At another man's request, he had labeled his own blood sample with that man's name. When the police questioned the young man, he told them whose name he had put on his blood sample. This person was arrested, and a sample of his blood was tested. The sample matched the DNA from the crime scene.

Indeed, the very fact that the assailant sought to avoid identification by having his name put on someone else's blood sample was strong circumstantial evidence of guilt. Such an act would have the same legal status as running away from the scene of a crime.

When the assailant was confronted with the DNA evidence, he confessed to both murders and was sentenced to life in prison. The criminal had quickly accepted DNA identification as positive proof of his guilt. In fact, however, the markers achieved by gel electrophoresis were questionable. By 1989, DNA evidence in several court trials in the United States and Australia had been excluded. Judges in these cases were not convinced that the tests were sufficiently accurate to support the pronouncement of severe penalties.

In these early instances, defense attorneys could reasonably question the precision of the tests. A nonmatch between the suspect's DNA and the residue from a crime scene could prove the suspect's innocence. However, a positive match does not always establish guilt. There is some small chance that two people have the same DNA pattern to the level at which it could be matched. For a time, prosecutors resorted to stating the odds of finding a more perfect match of DNA. They claimed, for example, that the odds of the match being positive were 10 million to one. Judges and juries do not like such statements.

The problem was gradually overcome by better technology. With the advances of profiling techniques, DNA identification is now as certain—actually, more certain—as identification obtained by matching fingerprints. Juries and judges have become accustomed to thinking of both fingerprints and DNA profiling as absolute indicators of identity. Defense attorneys now concentrate on how the sample materials were obtained, how they were stored and transported, and whether the person conducting the DNA testing is properly qualified. Cases can be won if doubts on these matters are raised in the minds of jurors. The science of DNA profiling, however, is no longer a serious issue.

Time, in a similar vein, has become a nonissue. Before the 1980s, the processes involved in chromatography and electrophoresis were tedious and time consuming. Now, much of the work is done by machines: a computer holds a large collection of standard blot patterns and compares them to the pattern of a sample of material. The most advanced techniques for analyzing DNA and RNA sequences use computerized machines to compare very small samples with thousands of standard patterns. The comparisons are so detailed and fast that sequences of thousands of DNA strands can be identified in less than one hour.

Other Applications of DNA Profiling

Now that DNA profiling has become reliable, inexpensive, and quick, many new applications have been advanced. For example, various commercial organizations have proposed DNA analysis for the identification of animals or animal remains. Samples of whale meat can be tested to determine whether the whale is on the list of endangered species.

Governments in various African countries are considering the use of similar methods to identify animals from herds in game preserves. Poachers frequently kill elephants and other large animals for their valuable tusks or horns. If DNA profiling could reveal the dead animal's previous preserve, authorities could increase surveillance in that park and better control the poaching.

Government officials in the United States have proposed that all military personnel be DNA-profiled and the records stored in a computer memory. Therefore, any former or present member of the military, dead or alive, could be easily identified. In addition, police have recommended that parents have their children profiled to facilitate identification in case of an accident, a fire, or abduction. So far, few parents have taken advantage of this practice.

DNA profiling would also prove helpful in the field of public health. The speed and accuracy in diagnosing the cause of an infection can be greatly improved. Both viruses and bacteria have highly species-specific DNA profiles. If the standard profiles of all known infectious agents were stored in computer memory, a sample of fluid from an infection can be identified in minutes.

Similarly, routine testing can detect bacterial food contamination quickly and inexpensively. The owners of several food processing plants have been required to destroy large amounts of condemned food. In some cases, the bad quality of the product was not discovered by a U.S. Food and Drug Administration agent until the food was packaged or shipped. If DNA profiling had been used in the initial stages of processing, the producers would have had an early warning and prompt actions would have saved time and money. Far more important, such methods might prevent outbreaks of food poisoning.

10
Biohazard

A biohazard is a material produced by a living organism that is a threat to humans or their environment. Research using disease germs or viruses can cause such a condition. Those involved in such research must use care at all times. Most living microorganisms employed in genetics research pose no biohazard or one that is moderate. Nevertheless, workers usually take precautions, such as wearing rubber gloves and surgical masks.

Scientists working with new organisms or new research techniques must be especially careful. No one is sure of the possible dangers. In the early 1970s, a new procedure caused scientists in biological research to pause, then proceed with caution. The new procedure was the creation of genetic hybrids. In this technique, strands of DNA from one species are linked to strands of DNA from a different species. After the dissimilar strands bond, this hybrid DNA can be transferred into the cells of a third organisms. By this transfer of hybrid DNA, one organism is given the inheritable characteristics from two other species. Scientists hoped that this innovation would lead to a better understanding of the causes of genetic disorders. They also sought practical applications in the treatment of disease.

Cancer Studies

President Lyndon B. Johnson declared war on cancer in 1965, and President Richard M. Nixon advanced the cause in the

1970s. The new funding allowed more research into the causes and cures of cancers. New projects were initiated and old projects were reinstated.

One new theory about the cause of cancer was based on the suspicion that certain cancers result from viral infections. This possibility was suggested by case studies of animal and human cancers. In some studies, cells removed from an animal's body were infected with viruses. Scientists saw that tumors developed in the animal when the infected cells were reintroduced into its body.

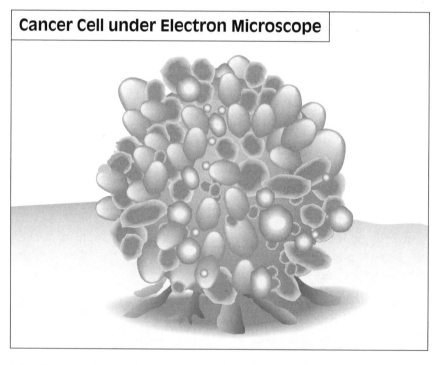

Cancer Cell under Electron Microscope

This drawing shows what a cancer cell might look like under an electron microscope. The cell is covered by small blister-like projections, the function of which is unknown. The cell is about 10 millimicrons—about 1/100,000 of an inch—in diameter.

A second line of research was focused on the possibility that some cancers have a hereditary origin. Again, case studies suggested that specific cancers tended to attack members of the same family. If a grandmother had breast cancer, the mother might develop breast cancer, and the daughters in the family were at risk. Most scientists involved in cancer research believed that a family's tendency toward certain cancers was an inherited characteristic.

In the early 1970s, Paul Berg was leading a program of basic cancer research at Stanford University in Palo Alto, California. His earlier successes included the use of viruses to transfer bacterial genes from one colony of bacteria to another. Using his methods of gene transfer, he hoped to determine whether some cancers are caused by hereditary factors and others by viral infections or, possibly, some combination of the two. In particular, he reasoned that the character of a human cell might be changed if invaded by a virus carrying a foreign gene. Consequently, Berg's initial goal was to determine whether a foreign gene could be introduced into a mammalian cell.

Using his recent research on gene transfer, Berg set out to build a stretch of DNA that contained genes from more than one species; in other words, he hoped to make a DNA hybrid. In order to keep the process as simple as possible, he worked on joining pieces of DNA from two different species of virus. One of the species naturally invades the bacterium *E. coli* and is commonly used in gene transfer studies. The second species of virus is often used to study viral infections in monkeys.

To begin the experiment, Berg obtained free-floating strands of DNA by using enzymes that dissolved the outer membranes of the two viruses. Another enzyme was used to cut the strands of DNA at certain places. When the DNA segments from the two types of viruses were mixed in the same beaker, some DNA strands from one type attached to strands from the other and formed a ring of DNA. This was the first time that DNA from two species had been joined outside a living cell. In 1980,

Berg won a Nobel Prize in chemistry for this work. The idea later become a cornerstone of genetic engineering.

Berg's next step was to move these rings of hybrid DNA into a living cell. Such rings, called "plasmids," can be absorbed through the cell wall of bacteria. If the bacteria *E. coli* were to be introduced into the beaker with the plasmids, some of the bacteria would likely absorb the hybrid plasmid. From then on, these bacteria would express the DNA from both viruses.

Unfortunately, Berg's careful project design had a flaw. Although one of the viruses was harmless, the virus used in monkey research had been known to induce cancer in laboratory animals. The virus was regarded as a biohazard.

Janet Mertz, one of Berg's advanced students, was assigned to carry out the stage of the project involving the transfer of DNA into the bacteria. She completed the arrangements but hesitated before actually inducing the transfer.

Mertz knew about the hazards of working with cancer-inducing viruses. Before taking the final step, she attended a course of cell-growing techniques at Cold Spring Harbor. Mertz described Berg's project to her instructor, Robert Pollack, who had worked with the monkey virus. Pollack believed that genes of dangerous viruses should not be used in the same studies with bacteria such as *E. coli*, which were able to survive in the human digestive system. Pollack and Mertz feared that a laboratory

Paul Berg was instrumental in generating the safety regulations covering research in recombinant DNA. (Courtesy of the National Library of Medicine)

worker might be accidentally infected with *E. coli* and that the virus genes in the *E. coli* could lead to a cancer. Another possibility was the accidental release of the bacteria into the environment. For example, the water used to wash a beaker could drain into the sewer system, which is a place that some *E. coli* find compatible.

When Mertz returned to Palo Alto, she informed Berg that she was reluctant to work with DNA from the questionable virus. At first, Berg was annoyed about Pollack's interference with his research program. He talked with Pollack on the telephone, but the problem was not resolved.

Berg next consulted several fellow scientists about the possible danger of his research. All urged caution because unknown factors were involved. Berg became uneasy about the technology of gene transfer and decided not to proceed with the planned experiment. Both the possible dangers of infection and his concerns about the methodology entered into the decision to stop the project. He believed that there were several other avenues open to resolve the problem. For example, he wanted to explore the prospects of finding a substitute for the monkey virus.

Steps Toward Wider Participation

Unknown to Berg, other researchers were investigating the role of viruses in the onset of cancer. Scientists at the National Institutes of Health (NIH) in Bethesda, Maryland, were involved in two separate projects. One was focused on the production of a viral chemical that might transform normal cells into cancer cells. Another was analyzing the mutations in the DNA of viruses. In addition, the scientists were searching for a specific segment of DNA that could lead to the development of tumors in animals.

During the late summer of 1971, these projects were discussed informally at a meeting at Cold Spring Harbor. The participants disagreed about the risk associated with the studies. Maxine Singer, a senior scientist working at the National Institutes of Health, proposed a set of safety recommendations. After the recommendations were documented, officials of the U.S. Department of Health and Human Services determined to make the safety regulations apply to all sections of the department, not just to the NIH. Many employees were unhappy with this decision. The resulting interagency arguments drew interest from outside the government.

When Berg heard about the concern of government officials, he and Singer organized a general conference on the topic. In January 1973, the conference, funded by NIH and the National Science Foundation, convened at the Asilomar Conference Center in Pacific Grove, California. The organizers arranged for research scientists to discuss their experiments with viruses that might cause cancer.

A follow-up discussion on the responsibility of working with biohazards was soon included in the agenda of another prestigious meeting. In the summer of 1973, the Gordon Conference on Nucleic Acids (DNA and RNA) was held in New Hampshire. Gordon Conferences are yearly events for a variety of scientific disciplines. Only the top people in each field are invited to attend the meetings. The agendas are always full, well in advance of the meeting dates. Consequently, there was no time set aside for a discussion of the hazards of hybrid DNA. However, because of its importance, one hour was added to the program for a discussion of the issues.

Although the discussion of possible hazards lasted only an hour, the scientists' discussion of their concerns was intense. The meeting was transcribed, and the resulting document was sent to the NIH officials.

Concern spread from centers such as Bethesda, Palo Alto, and Cold Spring Harbor. Leaders in genetic research realized that the community of biological scientists would need to

Scientists exchanging ideas at the Asilomar Conference of 1975 (Courtesy of the National Library of Medicine)

develop a common perspective on the hazards of DNA studies. Without this type of voluntary agreement, the government would certainly institute strict regulations and controls on such research.

Representatives of the mass media soon became aware of the controversy over biohazards. The public was informed and there were calls for extensive regulatory control over new genetic technology. The scientists became worried that such control would impede research progress. Consequently, the leaders in genetics and molecular biology proposed a second conference on the problems of biohazards. This meeting was also held at Pacific Grove and became known as the Asilomar Conference of 1975.

The goal was to formulate a set of reasonable rules that would encourage both safety and scientific progress. The participants formulated a scale to rank the risks generated by specific types of research. For example, the use of bacteria with a strong resistance to antibiotic medicines would be ranked as a high-risk procedure. The use of bacteria that could not live outside the laboratory would constitute a low risk.

The scientists established two types of safeguards. To prevent the spread of biohazards, high-risk research was to be conducted in isolated laboratories. During the experiments, workers would wear protective clothing and breathe through oxygen masks. Before leaving the laboratory, they would be decontaminated by disinfectant sprays. For less dangerous studies, workers would follow prescribed procedures for decontaminating themselves and their equipment.

In addition to these physical safeguards, a set of biological restraints was defined. For example, bacteria used in an experiment might be rendered unable to produce an essential vitamin; thereby making the bacteria unable to survive unless the specific vitamin was provided by research workers. In this way, if the bacteria escaped from the laboratory, it would soon die of vitamin deficiency.

The set of rules laid down at the Asilomar Conference of 1975 was sent to the NIH officials. These rules provided the basis for the federal regulation of genetic research. Most scientists and government officials agreed that the rules were strict but fair. While awaiting government action on the regulations, leading geneticists agreed to stop all questionable research.

The recess, or moratorium, on research was successful, but several procedural problems soon became evident. Administrators realized that the rules would be difficult to enforce. Agencies like NIH had no power to compel people to follow the regulations. They could, however, threaten to withdraw funding from those who did not comply. Since most of the basic research was conducted at universities and medical schools, such punishment could be effective.

Private industry was another matter. NIH had no control over private companies interested in genetic research. However, most major companies, such as pharmaceutical firms, voluntarily submitted to the new rules. Their administrators saw the necessity of maintaining good public relations.

Many members of the U.S. Congress were not satisfied with this initial arrangement. Many elected representatives believed that organizations such as the NIH should not be responsible for enforcing the new safety regulations. They worried that NIH officials would be too easy on the scientists they were funding. Some members of Congress believed that the federal government should pass legally enforceable legislation.

Donald Fredrickson, the director of the National Institutes of Health, saw a solution to these problems. He proposed the formation of advisory groups that could review and, perhaps, revise the decisions of officials who made research awards and formulated research policies. A committee of the National Academy of Sciences endorsed his plan. Coincidentally, the committee was chaired by Berg, whose project had sparked the need for regulations in genetic research.

Two advisory groups were formed. One was devoted to settling disagreements by reviewing and assessing the risk factors in disputed projects. The second group was set up to review the whole concept of the ethical responsibility of scientists and the implications of research for society as a whole. This group included leaders from all walks of life.

In the early 1970s, reports from the media and concerned scientists made the public aware of the ethical concerns (such as loss of privacy and discrimination based on DNA profiling) and health concerns (such as accidental biohazard releases into the environment) associated with genetic research. These concerns caused some local governments to pass ordinances restricting genetic research within their jurisdictional limits. In particular, Cambridge, Massachusetts, the home of Harvard University and the Massachusetts Institute of Technology—major research centers for biological science— enacted such laws.

Everyone looked to Washington, D.C., for guidance on this vital issue. When the federal rules from the NIH went into effect in 1975, members of Congress began to draft new laws to back up the regulations. Rather restrictive laws were soon proposed in both the House and the Senate. However, proponents of strict federal control of genetic research could not agree on major provisions. For example, they could not decide whether federal regulations should take precedence over local laws. After two years of arguments, the legislation on genetic research died a quiet death.

During that period, the need for restrictive laws had waned. A growing body of evidence revealed that there was little danger associated with the techniques of genetic research. In the beginning, uncertainty had fueled the feelings of fear, but an accumulation of scientific findings had diminished public anxiety.

Leading scientists learned many lessons from the long debates. They came to understand that the scientific community must be publicly accountable for genetic research and science in general. Scientists realized that when they explain their work in an intelligible manner, the public loses most of its fear of and hostility toward scientific research. Indeed, the experience showed that an informed public rarely withdraws support from the goals of basic science.

11

Clones

Newspaper accounts of cloning experiments read as if clones were exotic creatures from someone's wild imagination. Actually, clones are commonplace. Almost every potato plant is a clone (potatoes grown from seeds are a rare exception). Banana plants grown from root cuttings are clones. Pachysandra, a common broadleaved ground cover, produces underground runners. Each runner becomes a new plant that is a clone of the parent. Most bacteria, too, are natural clones.

In the language of genetics, *cloning* has three slightly different meanings. Basically, the process of cloning produces an organism that has the identical genetic makeup of the parent organism. Thus, a potato plant that grows from the bud, or eye, of the potato has the same DNA as the parent plant.

The second meaning comes from the fact that bacteria are natural clones. After a foreign gene has been inserted into a bacterium, the bacterium reproduces its own genetic material and that of the foreign gene. This material is carried into successive generations. Geneticists say that the foreign gene has been cloned by the bacteria.

The third meaning derives from the fact that a segment of DNA can be cloned outside the body of a plant or animal. The DNA segment is placed into a solution of nucleotides, submolecules formed from the pairing of one base submolecule and one of nucleic acid. Natural enzymes use the nucleotides to manufacture exact copies of DNA segments.

Animal Cloning

For some years, it has been possible to clone animals such as mice and white rats. For example, an egg is taken from a female mouse. The nucleus of that egg is removed with a tiny microsyringe and discarded. A pregnant mouse is chosen and a cell from her embryo is extracted. The nucleus is removed from the embryonic cell and inserted into the egg. The egg with the new nucleus is then placed in the womb of the egg-donor mouse. If the experiment is successful, the egg will develop into an infant animal and will be born in the normal manner. The animal will have the genetic makeup of the embryo donor, not that of the birth mother.

Sheep were among the first large mammals to be used in cloning studies. (Courtesy of the Agricultural Research Service of the U.S. Department of Agriculture)

While animal cloning has become relatively routine, the process continues to be laborious. The vast majority of attempted clones do not survive. Many of these fail because the embryonic cell is too mature. To achieve success, the cell and its nucleus must be extracted from the embryo during a very early state of development. Shortly after cell division is under way, the cells begin to develop into their specialized roles, such as skin cells or liver cells. If the embryo's cell is too mature when transplanted, cell division cannot proceed in the proper manner and a normal, viable infant will not be produced.

Recent experiments in Scotland have shown how to avoid this problem. Cells were extracted from the udder of a grown sheep. The cells were deprived of nutrition until the genetic material in their nuclei was inactivated. By starving the cells, the Scottish scientists forced the cells' nuclei to revert to an earlier stage of development. In this case, a functioning udder cell reverted to a completely undifferentiated cell. The nucleus of that now undifferentiated cell was removed, transplanted into an egg cell, and the egg implanted in the womb of the donor sheep. The cell began to divide and specialize in the normal manner. While this procedure seems somewhat fantastic, the proof was presented to the public in 1997 in the form of a living, eight-month-old lamb. This lamb is a clone of the sheep whose udder provided the cell nucleus and its DNA.

Scientists are planning to use this cloning technique to produce female sheep that will carry a human gene in their cells. Specifically, they hope to implant the human gene that directs the production of a blood-clotting enzyme, thrombin. This enzyme is missing in hemophiliacs; therefore, the blood of hemophiliacs does not clot or clots very slowly. In cases of an injury or surgical operation, these people might bleed to death without help.

If the geneticists are successful in introducing the gene for the blood-clotting enzyme into female sheep, the enzyme would appear in the sheep's milk. The cloned sheep can transmit the human gene to their offspring, and these offspring will produce the enzyme. Large flocks of the descendants of the clones could produce milk containing commercial quantities of the human blood-clotting enzyme. The enzyme can be extracted from the milk and purified for medical use. Such medicine could prolong the lives of hemophiliacs.

The cloning of large animals such as the Scottish sheep, produced strong reactions from scientists and the general public. The fear was raised that humans might be cloned by the same technique. While some infertile couples might wish to resort to cloning, the idea is repulsive to most people. The possibility of human clones as a source of organ transplants is also upsetting to many. Some members of the U.S. Congress have presented bills to prevent human cloning for any purpose.

Cloning at the Microbe Level

In contrast to larger animals, microbes tend to be natural clones. The parent cell divides into two daughter cells, which have the same genetic material as the parent. However, microbes can gain genetic material from other sources. From time to time, the tiny, single-celled microbes send out filaments to one another and exchange genetic material through these channels. Microbes also absorb free-floating genetic material through their cell walls.

Viruses also can carry nonviral genetic material into bacterial and other cells. For example, viruses that develop inside a microbe may accidentally incorporate some of the host's genetic material into their bodies. That material travels with the viruses when they invade another microbe. The material can be introduced into the genetic system of the new host.

Transmission of genetic material by simple absorption or by viral transfer has become a tool in genetic engineering. Bacteria, particularly *E. coli,* can be implanted with foreign genes. Genetic engineers have developed a method to determine whether the foreign genes are being expressed by the bacteria. They make a hybrid of the gene they want to implant and a gene that conveys immunity to a specific antibiotic. Only a few of the bacterial cells in a given colony may take in the hybrid genes, but those that do will survive and reproduce when the colony of bacteria is exposed to the antibiotic. The survivors can then be cultivated for use in other experiments.

Practical Applications

If organisms implanted with special-purpose genes can transmit them to their offspring, the availability of these genes and their protein products will be greatly improved. Scientists hope to utilize the genes to produce medicines in the form of proteins or enzymes.

The first human disease to be attacked by genetic methods was diabetes. Diabetes is a disease caused by a failure of the genes that regulate the production of insulin in the human pancreas. The pancreas is an organ attached to the digestive track that also provides many enzymes that aid digestion.

Physiologists knew by the early 1900s that sugar levels in the blood are controlled by material from the pancreas. However, the key hormone, insulin, was not isolated until 1922. The pure substance was produced by biochemists in 1926, but its composition was not determined until 1954 by the British scientist Frederick Sanger. Sanger's work led ultimately to the ability to produce human insulin by means of bacterial fermentation.

The bacteria *E. coli* were implanted with the human gene for the manufacture of insulin, and some of these implanted bacteria absorbed the new gene and began producing insulin. These particular bacteria were then cloned

A girl with diabetes, carefully giving herself an injection of insulin (Courtesy of the National Library of Medicine)

until there was a large population of billions of bacteria living in fermentation vats. The bacterial cells excrete human insulin into the broth as they continue to grow. Technicians remove portions of the broth at regular intervals. The insulin is extracted from the broth and purified to a crystalline form. When it is dissolved in pure saline water, the insulin can be injected into the bloodstream of a patient suffering from diabetes. It can then take the place of the insulin that is not being produced naturally because of a genetic defect in the patient.

Prior to the bacterial production of human insulin, animal insulin was used in the treatment of diabetes. Most such insulin was obtained from extracts of the pancreas of pigs. However, only a small amount of insulin could be obtained in this way, so there was a chronic shortage of insulin for the treatment of diabetics. Furthermore, many diabetic patients were allergic to pig insulin. Consequently, it was a major advance to be able to produce actual human insulin in large quantities through cloning.

12
Hereditary Disease

A ski resort in the Wasatch mountains of Utah was the setting where one of the keys to the intense study of hereditary disease clicked into place. The gathering in the spring of 1978 was for a ceremony that had taken place several times before. Every spring Mark Skolnick, a professor at the University of Utah, brought a small group of graduate students to the Alta ski resort to make presentations of their ongoing research to an audience of fellow researchers and two or three outside experts. The idea was to obtain high-level guidance in an informal setting on matters such as research techniques. The free exchange of scientific ideas was the main goal.

Skolnick was a population geneticist, and the principal line of discussion concerned matters such as the pattern of genetic abnormalities in large families. Utah is the headquarters of the Church of Jesus Christ of Latter-day Saints (Mormons). Their beliefs require the compilation of the careful records of kinship. Their archives of genealogy are world famous. Skolnick was allowed access to these archives when he was invited to join the faculty at the university. His initial focus had been on the prospect that these records could be computerized and that kinship connections could be determined very quickly and easily. However, he and his students had turned to looking for links to hereditary diseases.

Specifically, Skolnick's students were tracking a disease called hemochromatosis that is characterized by a failure of the body to rid itself of excess iron in the blood. They were seeking a possible link between the presence of this disease and the presence of one or more distinctive but harmless characteristics of the white cells in the blood. White blood cells produce antibodies, substances that are crucial to the body's normal defenses. Versions of this white blood cell factor vary slightly among groups of individuals. If the iron disease and one specific variation of the white blood cell factor were found together in same individual, the white blood cell factor might provide an early warning signal of the disease.

Skolnick's guests, in 1978, were two accomplished geneticists, David Botstein and Ronald Davis. When Kerry Kravitz, one of the research students, had finished his presentation, the two outside experts both saw immediate connections to work they were doing on the DNA of yeast cells. They were obtaining genetic profiles of the yeast cells by using chromatography.

It seemed possible to Botstein and Davis that people afflicted with a genetic disease might present a chromatographic profile pattern that could be connected to the disease. Specifically, a blotch in one particular location in the pattern of blotches might be seen in a victim's profile but not in the profile of a person unafflicted with a given disease. Such a blotch or set of blotches could then provide a marker for the disease.

Botstein and Davis suggested to Kravitz and Skolnick that their work might be much more accurate and cover many more inherited conditions if they tested the family members with whom they were working by using DNA chromatographic profiling rather than the protein from white blood cells. If the profiles did, indeed, yield specific disease markers, they might even begin to build a picture of the location of the gene that was causing the iron problem.

Genetic Markers

The idea of finding genetic markers opened the prospect of locating the gene for any of the inheritable conditions in the human species. The scientists thought that this might be done without even knowing the specific sequence of bases in the genes that made a person susceptible to a disease. They would simply be able to say, when this marker shows up, the chances are high that a gene with such and such a defect is present in the cells of this individual.

By using the techniques of crossover analysis developed by Morgan and his students, the scientists could gradually deduce which of the chromosomes was the home for a given marker. This was a very laborious process that required the chromatographic examination of many hundreds of samples of human DNA donated by many hundreds of volunteers, ideally from a single kinship group of cousins, aunts, uncles, and other close relatives.

Laborious as it was, the use of genetic markers was an attractive tool for the isolation and identification of the genes that were involved in hereditary diseases. When Botstein next attended a convention of geneticists, he found himself recommending the method to his fellow scientists. Among them was Ray White, who was then doing research at the University of Massachusetts on the DNA sequences of insects. White was soon enticed to test the effects of the restriction enzymes on human genetic materials. With the help of a postdoctoral student, Arlene Wyman, he found that the enzymes produced mixtures of pieces of DNA that were unique for each human. This was the first demonstration of DNA profiling.

The pattern of pieces of different lengths clearly showed contributions from both mother and father. That is, each parent's pattern of varied length fragments was partly mirrored in the offspring. This suggested that Botstein and Davis had been correct to suspect that such markers could be used to track inherited diseases across generations and provide indicators of the presence of a malfunctioning gene before the onset of the actual disease.

After the jointly authored paper on this discovery was published in 1979, White joined the faculty at the Howard Hughes Medical Institute, located at the University of Utah, where he could turn his talents to the job of relating more genetic markers to inherited diseases.

Huntington's Disease

Meanwhile, back in Massachusetts, the stage was being set for one of the great, emotional triumphs in the search for malfunctioning genes. The specific disability in question was Huntington's disease, a hereditary disease that leads to the gradual deterioration of the central nervous system. The key figure in tracking down the gene involved was Nancy Wexler. Wexler was trained originally in psychiatry but shifted career paths to neurology when it became obvious that her sister had developed Huntington's, the same condition that had killed their mother after years of mental and physical decline. Wexler was being helped by significant contributions from a charitable institution called the Hereditary Disease Foundation, Inc. It was established by the wife of Woody Guthrie, a folk singer who died of Huntington's. This effort was also supported by her father, who was successful as both a psychiatrist and a screenwriter for Hollywood films.

Wexler had been instrumental in finding a community in Venezuela where the incidence of Huntington's disease was extremely high. As early as 1976, officials of the National Institutes of Health recognized the significance of such a center of frequent occurrence of the disease and began to provide funds for Wexler to make extended trips to Venezuela.

In villages around Lake Maracaibo (actually a nearly land-locked bay of the Caribbean Sea) there was an intermarried population of about 2,500 people, nearly 100 of whom had symptoms of Huntington's. For such a rare disease, this was an unusual find. Wexler had the chore of explaining to these people that she and her colleagues were seeking a deeper understanding of the disease that plagued them—and that to do so, she needed samples of their blood.

The next step toward tracking down the Huntington's gene was brought about by a molecular biologist named David Housman. His laboratory was near Botstein's at the Massachusetts Institute of Technology. Botstein, White, and Housman were brought together with Wexler at a seminar sponsored by the charitable foundation. Botstein, one of the originators of the genetic marker idea, and Housman did not agree on how the Venezuelan villagers' blood samples could contribute to advancing knowledge. Botstein wanted to conduct an extensive genetic survey of the DNA of as many villagers as possible. Housman wanted to focus on people who had the malfunctioning gene but did not yet show symptoms of the disease. In particular, Housman hoped to find some people who had inherited such a malfunctioning gene from both the father and the mother. If such a doubly victimized individual could be found, it opened up the prospect of discovering precisely which gene was at fault, what the fault was, and where the gene was located—the exact spot on a particular chromosome. Housman was thinking about a direct attack on the disease rather than basic research on the question of the role of genetic markers.

Housman teamed up in a collaboration with medically oriented colleagues at the Massachusetts General Hospital in submitting a request for funding to the NIH. By this time, Wexler was working as a field researcher for the National Institute of Neurological Diseases and Stroke within the NIH. She convinced her supervisors that she should be a participant

4874
4875
4773
4214
4218
4230
4454
4202
4451
4571
4610
4611
4616
4616
4876
4142
4225
4224

One of the first genetic profiles produced by chromatographic analysis (Courtesy of the Huntsman Cancer Institute, University of Utah)

in the Housman study. In part because of her family experiences with Huntington's and in part because she was herself at risk for developing the disease, the scientific search for the marker and the gene, itself, became a crusade. After almost four years and the passage of scientific leadership from David Housman to Michael Conneally, a valid marker was found. By late spring 1983, the gene at fault could be localized on chromosome number 4. However, there was no progress toward a cure for the disease.

During the same time period and quite independently, some similar work was going forward in England. There, the focus was on sickle-cell anemia and other hereditary flaws in the red blood cells. Sickle-cell anemia is a chronic blood disease in which some of the red blood cells become crescent-shaped and impede the normal flow of blood in small blood vessels. It mainly afflicts people of African descent. The flaw in the hemoglobin protein that caused sickle-cell anemia had long since been identified by the American chemist Linus Pauling, so there was no question that the disease was hereditary and caused by the reversal of one particular nucleotide near one end of the gene. The search for a genetic marker was mounted by Sir Walter Bodmer and an American research worker, Ellen Solomon. Their work resulted in the discovery of a marker for sickle-cell anemia in 1979.

Other Genetic Disorders and Responses

Twenty-five years later, 95 different medical conditions had been proven to have a genetic origin. These conditions range from male pattern baldness, a non-life-threatening condition, to varieties of leukemia that are almost always fatal. Understanding the genetic aspects of some of these conditions—including causes and possible treatments—has been difficult. For many, precise knowledge of the faulty gene has not led to a certain cure or a more effective treatment.

One example of this problem is the quest for understanding amyotrophic lateral sclerosis (ALS), also known as Lou Gehrig's disease. The disease is characterized by a gradual loss of muscular control. Microscopic examination shows a deterioration of the nerves that activate the voluntary muscles. The onset typically occurs around the age of 50, when affected nerve cells begin to wither and eventually die. Lou Gehrig, the famed baseball player, showed the first signs of the disease much earlier—in his mid-30s. He died in 1941, at age 39, a few years after he had retired from his amazing career in baseball. It is ironic that Gehrig, known as the "Iron Man" of baseball, suffered from a disease that eventually devastated the muscles of his athletic body. During his career, he maintained top batting averages and home run records. Indeed, his uninterrupted string of starts for the New York Yankees was 2,130. This record was unbroken until 1998, when Cal Ripken of the Baltimore Orioles achieved 2,632 consecutive starts for his team.

The publicity surrounding Gehrig's tragic fate increased the efforts to understand the cause of the condition. Researchers looked for infectious agents such as bacteria and viruses. No such link was found. Early on, there was some suspicion of a genetic connection because a family pattern of the illness had been observed. The link was ambiguous because the children of ALS victims rarely showed the disease and seemed to live normal life spans. The genetic connection proved to be more common among relatives such as cousins. Sometimes the disease would skip a generation and the victim's grandchild would show symptoms although the parents were unaffected. Most often, however, there was no familial connection at all.

One promising line of inquiry held that ALS was somehow akin to cancer. The deteriorated nerve cells of ALS victims seemed to exhibit an internal malfunction similar to the malfunction of cancer cells. Scientists hypothesized that ALS was, like many cancers, caused by the interaction of an environmental toxin (such as tobacco smoke) and a broad genetic susceptibility.

However, anthropologists reported that ALS-type symptoms existed among isolated tribes living in the Tropics. By 1961, it was apparent that natives of Guam showed an abnormally high incidence of ALS-type diseases. These observations, however, could not be connected to research on environmental toxins until the 1990s. At that time, neurotoxic effects were observed in laboratory mice fed seeds of the cycad tree, a staple in the Guamian diet. The mice gradually lost muscular control over their hind limbs. This muscular deterioration mimicked human symptoms related to ALS diseases. The toxic material was identified as a molecule named BMAA, which is produced by the bacteria living in the roots of the cycad tree. The toxic material generated by the roots contaminates the entire tree—including the edible seeds. The Guamians, however, always subjected the seeds to a high temperature as they prepared their food—soups, stews, or bread baked with cycad seed flour. The heat destroyed most of the BMAA, and the dietary concentration of BMAA appeared to be too low to cause the symptoms of ALS. Nevertheless, research on the dangers of BMAA was continued.

In 2003, a team of anthropologists from the National Botanical Gardens in Hawaii discovered a more promising dietary pathway for the BMAA. The Guamians prize flying squirrels as food. The squirrels are known to eat cycad seeds and insects that feed on other contaminated tree parts. Although the animals are cooked whole in coconut milk, the high concentration of BMAA found in the squirrels' bodies was deemed to be sufficient to cause the ALS symptoms. This discovery fits in with other prominent theories of the cause of ALS—the ingestion or inhalation of environmental toxins.

Evidence from ALS research points to materials containing active oxygen—such as the ozone found in smog or electrically charged environments (the air after a thunderstorm) as the possible causes of nerve cell deterioration. When vitamin E or other antioxidants, such as lycopene, found in tomatoes, or lutein, from yellow squash, are included in the diet of laboratory animals, the decline of nerve cells can be slowed. To study the effects of antioxidants, officials of the U.S. Food and Drug Administration have approved the use of selenium, found in copper ore, and certain zinc compounds for tightly controlled human experiments.

Now that all the base pairs in the human genome have been identified and located on specific chromosomes, medical researchers have found a widening genetic role in ALS. At first, an apparent link to the disease was traced to chromosome 22. Then, another connection was found in chromosome 2. The X (female) chromosome was also identified as a carrier of a mutated gene. At last count, nine gene locations were considered as possible sites for the abnormal genes that can cause ALS.

All the studies of ALS suggest that this condition can have multiple causes. A variety of environmental conditions—including specific toxic materials, such as exposure to the lead in some paints—works in conjunction with a variety of separate genetic mutations to produce a set of symptoms known as ALS. Therefore, cures for this disease may need to be tailored to the particular pattern of causes of the condition for each victim.

A ray of hope is provided by the case of another famous person with ALS. Stephen Hawking, the renowned astrophysicist, was diagnosed as having the disease when he was only 21 years old. Most victims die of ALS within a few years of its onset. However, Hawking, a quadriplegic, is in his sixties and holds the position of Lucasian Professor of Mathematics at Cambridge University. Sir Isaac Newton once held this same position in 1663. In addition to Hawking's production of scientific papers, he has written two best-selling, nontechnical books on cosmology for nonphysicist readers. Hawking is married and has three children and one grandchild. He has been aided by colleagues in overcoming the problems related to his disabilities. Friends at the Massachusetts Institute of Technology designed and assembled the computerized equipment that allows Hawking to communicate at a speed similar to his speech pattern before he was stricken with the disease.

ALS is a frightening condition that has complicated genetic roots and no apparent cure. However, some, like Hawking, fight through their disability and lead an enjoyable life.

Another frightening genetic disease is cancer of the retina—called retinoblastoma (RB). It is particularly an emotion-arousing condition because it often strikes very young children. Journalists publicized the disease when the baby of popular TV actors developed RB. Unfortunately, routine examinations did not uncover the cause of the problem and the child was diagnosed as having a less dangerous eye condition. Such an incorrect diagnosis is very dangerous because cancer cells from the eye can migrate to other parts of the body. The unchecked cancer is often fatal. In this case, the child recovered after one eye was surgically removed. New techniques can now control all but the most advanced cases of RB. Medicines such as vincristine—from the rosy periwinkle—focused radiation, and laser surgery now save the sight of many young RB victims.

Fortunately, RB is relatively rare. Studies have shown that only 1 in 20,000 children born in the United States will develop the disease. In 10 percent of cases, the condition is directly inherited, but in all cases, some genetic involvement has been recognized. The key to the disease is a protein composed of over 900 amino acid units. This protein provides one of the bodily controls of cell replication, and when unable to function properly, cells in the eye multiply at a runaway pace and cancer is the result.

The gene that initiates the production of the growth-control protein is located on chromosome 13 and was first identified in 1996. At about the same time, a new theory attempted to explain the unusual pattern of genetic involvement in RB cases. The theory proposes that a baby would not develop RB if one parent provided a normal gene and the other a mutated gene. According to this hypothesis, one healthy gene could produce sufficient growth-control protein. The theory also proposed that RB could develop a few months after birth if a second additional mutation occurred at the same time that the baby's retina was going through a normal growth spurt. Although some medical evidence appeared to confirm this idea, the latest research has found similar growth-control genes on seven other chromosomes. Therefore, a direct cause of RB remains uncertain.

Today scientists are aware that the body has many different control systems for regulating the growth of various cells. While there is probably some duplication in the systems, there is also some specialization. Thus, the growth-control protein triggered by the gene on chromosome 13 might regulate retinal cells exclusively. However, it is possible that the protein might also control biochemically similar cells in other bodily organs. This hypothesis could help explain why victims of RB seem to have a tendency to develop other types of cancer.

In any case, it is increasingly apparent that the control mechanisms in the human body are highly complicated and often include duplicate functions.

Further Genetic Therapy Research

Since the recent advances in gene identification, some journalists have suggested the existence of an ongoing revolution in both medical research and the application of such research in the provision of health care. This opinion, however, appears somewhat too optimistic. Although scientists now understand the links between certain diseases and specific genes, only a little can be done with the knowledge. At present, most gene therapy remains in the laboratory stage and some human test trials have not gone well. Indeed, the concept of genetic medicine has raised more questions than answers. The use or misuse of genetic information is the basis of many such questions.

The basic idea in genetic therapy is to replace or silence a malfunctioning gene. Sometimes the malfunction means that a vital protein or enzyme is not being produced and the gene needs to be replaced. Sometimes the malfunctioning gene is producing a protein or enzyme that is actively harmful. Such genes must be silenced if the patient is to regain health.

Both situations require that new genetic material be introduced into specific cells in the patient's body. In the standard method, viruses are used as carriers. They are modified by the removal of their disease-causing capabilities. New genetic material is then introduced and the virus carriers are injected into the patient's bloodstream or diseased organ. The viruses enter the targeted cells and implant the new genetic material.

These procedures were successfully tested on laboratory animals, and the U.S. Food and Drug Administration approved using the method on human subjects. In 1999, a male teenager died while the human test trials were underway. The young man suffered from a life-threatening condition in which the process that rids the body of excess nitrogen had ceased to function properly. His body was unable to transform the nitrogen into urea, and ammonia built up in his blood. The toxic ammonia impaired normal nerve function and the patient was losing all control of his body. In danger of dying from the disease, the young man volunteered to test the new genetic therapy.

The patient's doctors sought to replace the gene that guides the manufacture of an enzyme crucial to the process of nitrogen elimination. All went well for a few days. On the fourth day, the patient died of what was seen to be a massive antibody reaction to the viruses that carried the life-saving replacement gene.

One such death could have been a twist of fate. However, in 2003, a child in a similar gene therapy program conducted in France suffered a breakdown in white blood cell functions and developed leukemia. As in the earlier case, a massive antibody reaction was blamed for the disaster. This event led the Food and Drug Administration, which monitors the development of new therapeutic procedures, to ban such tests until better safety measures could be brought to bear.

Problems experienced during human clinical trials have not deterred the scientists who test laboratory animals or microorganisms. Additional research has demonstrated that some of the new techniques and approaches can be both safe and effective. Among these new approaches is the use of single genes, gene fragments, or RNA fragments. Such tiny bits of genetic material can interfere with the production of proteins or enzymes and are more safely introduced into the cells of laboratory animals than microbes. Scientists hope that smaller, less dangerous carriers will supplant the use of the troublesome and sometimes deadly viruses.

In one new approach, minute globules of fat are used to carry a single gene or gene fragment into the interior of target cells. This method of gene insertion takes advantage of the fact that a major component of an animal cell membrane is composed in part by fat-like molecules akin to cholesterol. The miniature globules of fat used as a carrier of genetic material are therefore more easily accepted by the cell membranes than viral or watery carriers. Experiments using this technique have been conducted on mice suffering from a condition similar to cystic fibrosis, the most common disease of genetic origin. Cystic fibrosis is caused when a damaged gene produces a specific protein that causes a thick gummy layer of mucus to form in the victim's air passages. The patient then suffers from serious breathing difficulties. If undamaged genes or genetic suppressors can be inserted into the cells that line the nose, trachea and lungs, the disease can be controlled. Experiments with mice used a nasal mist of tiny fat particles containing copies of the good, undamaged gene. Researchers found that the gene carriers in the nasal mist did not penetrate every cell of the nasal lining. They also determined that the proper protein was not produced by every cell-penetrating gene. However, enough penetrations were successful and enough of the new genes were able to function so that the corrected cells were able to significantly reduce the disease symptoms and the animal could breathe more easily.

Similar techniques using RNA rather than DNA are being tried on laboratory animals showing diseases such as Huntington's disease and Parkinson's disease. Both are caused by the malfunction of cells in the central nervous system. For these conditions, the medical goal is again to quiet the gene that produces a malformed or toxic protein. The presence of this gene results in the victim's loss of higher mental functions—such as muscular control. In tests of the technique, the microscopic fat particles containing small segments of RNA are injected into the blood of laboratory animals. Capillaries transport the particles into the brain. Here, the fatty containers penetrate both the capillary walls and nerve cell membranes, and the RNA enters the targeted nerve cells. This new genetic material then shuts down the damaged gene.

Experiments using the miniaturization technique have been done where fragments of DNA or RNA are injected directly into the target tissue without the use of a carrier. This technique has been tried on mice that have a condition similar to macular degeneration—a disorder of the sensory cells at the center of the retina that provide fine visual acuity. To combat this condition, a tailored fragment of RNA is injected directly into the retina. The new RNA interferes with the transmission of the harmful enzyme sent by the mutated and malfunctioning gene. Thus, the harmful enzyme is silenced. In recent tests of this method, visual acuity has been partially restored. While this new type of gene therapy appears to work reasonably well in mice, much more research is needed before such procedures can be tried on human subjects.

13

Genomes

Genome is the name given to the totality of DNA molecules in each bodily cell of an organism. Each egg or sperm cell—the reproductive cells of an organism—contains one-half of the full genome. (When the egg and sperm unite, the full genome is achieved.) During the time between 1980 and 1985, the idea of sequencing the whole human genome was being discussed at scientific meetings and in academic laboratories around the United States and in other countries such as Britain and Japan.

The idea was not always welcomed. Many biological scientists were worried that the cost of such a venture would be so high that all the small, individual research projects would be dropped from the budgets of the government agencies from which support normally came.

Some of the enthusiasm for such a project came from universities whose administrators were seeking a quick pathway to world-class status by attracting top researchers with money from the federal government. Some government officials had even stronger motives for pushing such a project. For example, by 1985, justification for a continually increasing role in scientific research for the U.S. Department of Energy (DOE) was waning. The scientific resources under the department's direct control were threatened with cutbacks in budget and personnel.

Many of the scientists employed in the network of national laboratories supported by the department were skilled in molecular biology and genetics. In particular, work had proceeded for 40 years on studies of the effects of nuclear radiation on genetic material. This research experience was seen as vital to the efficient operation of massive DNA sequencing.

Coincidentally, a second significant Alta meeting took place in December 1984. This meeting was called by officials of the DOE and a branch of the World Health Organization concerned with environmental causes of mutations and cancers. The topic was the detection of mutations in the generation of Japanese children who had been born after the nuclear explosions at Hiroshima and Nagasaki in 1945. The upshot of this meeting, which was attended by Ray White and David Botstein, was that available methods of detecting mutations were totally inadequate for making precise measurements of changes in the rate of mutation due to unusual environmental conditions. The scientists concluded that only by knowing the composition of every human gene could sufficient accuracy be obtained. At the time, no one thought that such a feat would be possible—but the seed had been planted.

The other government agency with a special interest was the NIH. In particular, a genome mapping activity fit into the strategy for waging war on cancer, since medical scientists had come to believe strongly that most cancers had a hereditary aspect if not a direct cause. Such ideas generated support in many sectors of the biomedical community. For example, Renato Dulbecco, a Nobel Prize winner and president of the Salk Institute (for medical research), began a crusade in favor of the project in the spring of 1986. Soon others chimed in. Studies were mounted at the request of congressional committees by the staff of the Office of Technology Assessment, which at that time provided scientific advice to the Senate and the House of Representatives. The results of these studies supported the medical value of sequencing the human genome. Likewise, a panel directed to review the prospect was formed by the National Academy of Sciences and directed by staff of the National

James Wyngaarden, as director of the National Institutes of Health, helped persuade the U.S. Congress to support the Human Genome Project. (Courtesy of the National Library of Medicine)

Research Council. The panel was required to assess the prospective costs and benefits of having a complete map of the human genome. The mission was to clarify the scientific issues and hold back on the public policy and political factors until the science had been made clear to all who held a stake in the prospective effort. Again, the recommendations were favorable.

Ultimately, the mounting of such a project required the approval of the U.S. Congress and the appropriation of funds. James Wyngaarden, director of the NIH, carried the conclusions of the various studies into congressional hearings. He obtained the first small budgetary allowance ($3.85 million) for planning to be done in 1988. The following year, the amount rose to $28 million, and it has been increasing ever since.

In 1988, the NIH and the DOE agreed to work together on the Human Genome Project. The agencies needed to show a common front to congressional committees. The agreement forestalled a breakdown in the funding momentum. Progress would have been retarded if the agencies had expended their energies in rivalry rather than cooperation. In the actual mounting of the project—based in part on the advice of many deliberative bodies such as the National Academy of Sciences—the leadership role was given by Congress to the NIH.

Polymerase Chain Reactions

The main technology that initially engendered the sequencing of the entire human genome was DNA profiling. Profiling works best when there are many copies of each DNA fragment. If small samples of DNA could be copied somehow, the whole process would be made more efficient and more accurate.

Cloning genes or other known stretches of DNA in the bodies of bacteria worked reasonably well. However, biochemists and molecular biologists sought a method for cloning the stretches of DNA more rapidly and without the mess of fermentation tanks and the apparatus needed to grow large numbers of bacteria or yeast cells.

The polymerase chain reaction (PCR) is the means by which sample stretches of DNA are now cloned. The process involves chopping long DNA strands into pieces of various lengths by the use of restriction enzymes. These enzymes cut DNA at very specific sites and only at such sites. The resultant DNA "soup" is heated above 170° Fahrenheit (about 77° Celsius) to make the double strands of DNA separate. A technical worker then introduces a different enzyme, known as a polymerase, and a plentiful supply of the nucleotides that are the elemental units of DNA. A polymerase enzyme stitches DNA units into a chain. The enzyme gathers up free-floating submolecules of DNA and clamps them onto the original stretches of DNA to form new complementary stretches.

When the solution is heated again, the new double strands of DNA uncouple. The solution is cooled and the polymerase enzyme that does the actual copying is added afresh. When it has done its work, the number of complete strands is doubled.

If there were 100 identical single strands of DNA separated in the original soup, the polymerase enzyme would fill in the complements to the open strands, using the loose submolecules in the watery solution as raw material. Then there would be 100 double stands of DNA. When the solution is reheated, the paired strands will come apart again and the process will repeat—making 200 double strands. The cycle can be continued until there are millions of identical paired strands. Each of the paired strands is a clone of the original.

The polymerase chain reaction was invented by Kary Mullis, a biochemist who worked for one of the new genetic engineering companies that were springing up in settings such as the San Francisco Bay region and near the NIH in Bethesda, Maryland. Mullis was and is what some people call a free spirit. He received his flash of inspiration while on a moonlit motorcycle ride. After his insight, he had a series of disagreements with his coworkers and employers about how the invention was to be communicated to the larger scientific community. The situation became sufficiently confused so that Mullis's name did not appear on the first published report of the PCR process. In spite of this initial oversight, Mullis was awarded the Nobel Prize in chemistry in 1993 for his invention.

The construction of new strands of DNA took several hours using the Mullis technique. Most of the time was taken by the heating and cooling of the solution. Also, after one cycle, the copying, polymerase, enzyme had to be replaced because it was destroyed by the heat. However, the technique was greatly accelerated when new enzymes were discovered in the bacteria that live in hot springs, such as those found in Yellowstone Park.

With the heat-resistant enzymes, a PCR cycle could be completed in a few minutes by a computer-controlled machine. Each cycle would double the number of replicas of the known stretch of DNA. If the process was started with a single strand, a four-hour process could produce millions of copies. After such large numbers of identical strands of DNA became available, the goal of characterizing all the bases in human DNA and locating specific genes in such sequences was brought closer to reality.

The Human Genome Project

Minor disputes about the direction of the project continued. For example, there were disagreements between traditional geneticists and those representing the field of molecular biology. The molecular biologists were sometimes seen as having greater interest in the commercialization of genetic engineering than in basic research. Officials of the NIH wished to show that their goal was to further basic research rather than to support the development of new products—even when such products might have a direct role in improved medical treatments.

Three decisions on the part of the top officials of the NIH tended to quiet the controversy. First, they chose James Watson as project director. Watson, with Francis Crick, had found the correct structure of the DNA molecule. The naming of Watson as director signaled to the various research

Human Chromosome Pair

Note: The pattern of stripes is consistent in all humans. The stripes help in localizing specific genes.

A representation of the largest human chromosome (number 1). As can be seen in the diagram, the other member of the paired set has a similar banded appearance. This is one pair of the 22 standard pairs humans have in addition to the pair of gender-directing chromosomes (the X and the Y).

communities that the leaders of NIH wanted a person in charge of the project who was a specialist in molecular biology but who stood for fundamental research.

The second move was to divide the project into segments that could be funded to the benefit of many different institutions. The project managers did this by assigning specific chromosomes to the various academic laboratories where the labeling and sequencing work would be done. This indicated to the workers that there was serious interest in the whole genomic structure, not just the genes that were possibly involved in hereditary diseases.

The message of the third decision was similar. That decision set aside funds to investigate the genomes of organisms other than humans. Such work had already begun before the official start of the genome project in 1990. Now it was extended to more species, including many plants as well as animals and bacteria. The complete genomes have been mapped for several microbes such as *E. coli* and the bacterium that causes the serious disease anthrax. A complete genome has also been established for yeast cells.

The ultimate goal of the project, however, is to identify each DNA molecule found in each human chromosome and characterize the sequence in which the DNA molecules are organized. The result would be a diagram showing the recipe for each of the proteins and RNA molecules necessary to sustain life.

The decision to sequence the human genome was not made lightly. Science administrators in the DOE, the NIH, and other government bodies knew that the project would mean many years of intense work and would cost billions of dollars. To reduce the amount of time and money spent on the project, the leaders brought in a number of research institutions from around the world. The International Human Genome Sequencing Consortium is composed of 20 research centers in six countries, each of which has been assigned a list of

The office and laboratory building of the European Bioinformatics Institute, where computerized records of genome sequences are made accessible to the research community. The institute is part of the Sanger Institute complex near Cambridge University in England. (Courtesy of EBI staff)

chromosomes to study. This was a convenient, if somewhat arbitrary way to divide up the task.

Initially, most of the administrators imagined that the work would become easier as the project went forward. They anticipated that technological advances would speed up the process and that the teams of scientists would become more efficient. They were correct.

A draft version of the complete human genome was ready in 2001—about five years ahead of the original schedule. The "final" version was completed in 2003. The quotation marks signify that the total job, however, is really incomplete. By mid-2005, only about 20,000 genes had been positively identified. Researchers believe that there may be 5,000 to 10,000 as yet unidentified genes located throughout the genome.

In addition, a unitary diagram of a single genome is not sufficient to cover the topic. Some consideration must be given to the likelihood that there are significant differences in the genomes of men and women. Variations may also be found on a regional and ethnic basis. Similarly, some attention must be paid to variations among individuals. The existing diagram is, in fact, a composite of the genomes from several individuals who represent several different ethnic backgrounds.

Researchers were careful to assure the anonymity of the persons who contributed their DNA; nevertheless, one source is known. J. Craig Venter, the head of the Celera Genomics, revealed that some of his DNA was present in the sample processed by his own firm. In the initial plan, sequencing was to be done in either government laboratories or laboratories affiliated with a university. However, Celera Genomics is a commercial firm and their involvement received no financial support from the government.

The participation of Venter came about in an interesting way. He began his involvement with biomedicine as a Navy medical corpsman in the Vietnam War. Upon his release from service, he enrolled in the University of California at San Diego and in six years completed both his undergraduate and graduate studies in physiology and pharmacology. These interests led him to a job with the NIH, where his research assignment was in the area of molecular biology. Frustrated with the pace of his progress and a lack of administrative support, he decided to use his own money to purchase a key piece of computerized sequencing equipment.

Venter rapidly sequenced just those sections of human DNA that contained active genes (a small fraction of the total genome, which consists mainly of inactive DNA). This success led to some disagreements with the managers of the NIH section of the genome project. Venter's discontent resulted in his decision to leave the NIH. Aided by financial backing from the Perkin-Elmers Corporation, a major biochemical producer,

Venter founded The Institute for Genomic Research (TIGR). He and his colleagues soon announced that they had fully sequenced the genome of the medically important bacterium *E. coli*. This success allowed him to attract capital investment from additional commercial sources, and Celera Genomics was founded. Venter and his associates believed that various pharmaceutical houses would purchase his information on genetic materials.

Venter's idea that some genomic information might become private property spurred government officials to speed up their efforts to complete their sequencing projects. These officials, unlike Venter's group, wanted the outcome of genomic research to become public property and to be freely available to all those who might benefit from the information. Over the following years, competition was rife between the academic and government laboratories on one side and Celera's commercially oriented scientists on the other. Although some gaps remained in their findings, Venter's group may have finished the race in first place. Celera's commercial orientation, however, had annoyed many scientists. To avoid any problems, both sides declared that the race was a tie.

The Human Genome

The human genome has a total of approximately 3 billion nucleotides. Each nucleotide is one tiny link in a DNA chain and is composed of a sugar molecule, a base molecule, and a phosphorus atom. Within the nucleus of a bodily cell, a human DNA chain of nucleotides is organized into 46 separate strands. Each of the strands is wound around one of the 46 chromosomes (22 pairs plus the two gender genes) that make up most of the human genome. Each chromosome, which contains several thousand genes, consists of a protein core. This core acts as the foundation upon which the DNA is wound—somewhat like thread wound around a spindle.

The present estimate of the number of active human genes is about 30,000. A typical gene is composed of about 1,500 nucleotides. These tiny nucleotides hold the sequences of DNA that supply the recipes for proteins, the building blocks of all bodily organs. However, only 45 million nucleotides (out of the estimated 3 billion nucleotides) are contained in the 30,000 active genes. Therefore, the figure of 30,000 active genes represents about 2 percent of the total number of genes in the human genome. In other words, 98 percent of the human genome contains so-called junk DNA.

In addition to the apparent shortage of active genes, scientists are trying to solve a parallel puzzle: There are only about 30,000 genes but at least 50,000 different types of proteins in the human body. If, as scientists have speculated, one gene is required for each protein recipe, thousands of genes would seem to be missing. It is possible that the products of the active genes can be mixed and matched in various combinations to generate a variety of composite proteins. Some very large proteins are known to be composites, and it is likely that the completion of other large proteins requires the presence of more than one gene type.

The purpose of the 98 percent of the genome that contains no active genes is still ambiguous. Researchers believe that some seemingly inactive portions of the genome are responsible for activating or deactivating transient genes, such as those that are active only during various stages of growth or other bodily changes. These transient genes include those responsible for the onset of puberty or adjustments to the immune system during the invasion of infectious agents. If these suppositions are true, the changes in gene activity during the various stages in growth could be partially explained. Similarly, adaptations to bodily changes could be more easily monitored. Other gene segments may contain the signals that begin or end the copying of nucleotides. Some of the spare DNA is probably composed of ancient and obsolete genes that have been retired and are slowly breaking up. Conversely, some of the DNA could be the assembly ground for the development of new genes.

The difficulty in locating active genes among the long stretches of inactive DNA may account for some of the ostensibly missing genes. The real (active) genes usually contain within themselves short strands of inert DNA that tend to mask their actual status. These inert sections are called introns, and their function is somewhat mysterious. Indeed, the full consequences of sequencing the human genome will not be easily or quickly realized.

Comparative Genomics

In addition to the human genome, those of 190 other creatures have been initially sequenced. The information gained from these investigations is very helpful because biomedical researchers almost always use animals as test subjects for new medicines. Indeed, sometimes a whole series of animals—from mice, rats, and dogs to pigs, monkeys, and chimpanzees—is used in making the evaluation of one drug. Therefore, it is helpful to know animal physiology, including the genetic makeup of each test animal.

Research on the genomes of microorganisms is also important. Many microbes are agents of infection and the research enables new medicines to be tested. Other microbes are themselves potential sources of medicines; for example, penicillin, a leading antibiotic, was discovered while investigating the properties of bread mold, a common microorganism.

Economic benefits and pure scientific curiosity are other reasons to pursue research on nonhuman genomes. Sequencing the corn genome, for example, provided leads that have made the corn plant more resistant to disease and therefore more cost efficient. The finding that some genes are shared among humans and all other species helps define humankind's place in nature. Specific examples can illuminate how the nonhuman genome projects have helped medical advances, aided economic decisions, and solved long unanswered questions.

CAENORHABDITIS ELEGANS

Caenorhabditis elegans is a tiny gray-white nematode, a type of cylindrical worm, about as big as the letter *e* in this text. The organism is easily sustained in the laboratory, multiplies rapidly, and completes its life cycle in two to three weeks. When a

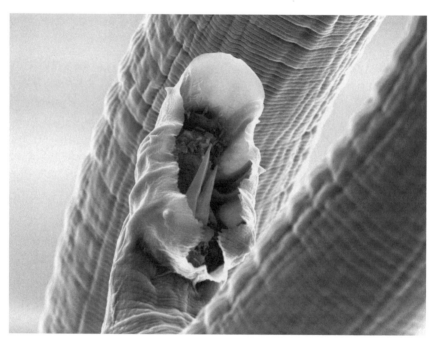

A prize-winning photo from an image provided by an electron microscope of the tail section of a male C. elegans *nematode* (Courtesy of David H. Hall, Center for *C. elegans* Anatomy, Albert Einstein College of Medicine, Bronx, New York)

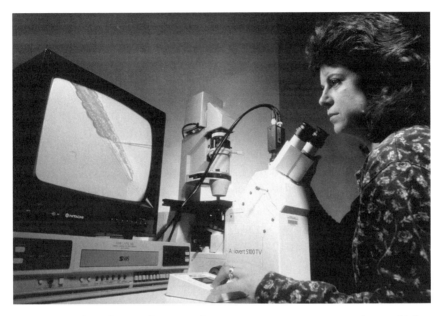

An image of C. elegans *from an electron microscope presented on a high-resolution TV screen* (Courtesy of the Agricultural Research Service of the U.S. Department of Agriculture)

particularly interesting strain—such as a special mutation—appears in the lab, specimens can be frozen with liquid nitrogen, held for long time periods, and then revived.

In 1962, Sydney Brenner, a South African biologist, was looking for a new direction in genetic research. He hoped to develop a program of study that would have been impossible before the 1953 discovery of DNA. While at Cambridge University, Brenner discussed his ideas in molecular biology with Francis Crick, a codiscoverer of the DNA molecule. Soon, Brenner decided to study the embryonic development of the nervous system and looked for the simplest creature with such a system. The nematode *C. elegans* was the perfect organism for his research.

C. elegans has two sexes: male and bisexual. At maturity, the worm is composed of a small number of reproductive cells and only 959 bodily cells, of which 300 are nerve cells. The relatively small number of cells in the complete organism allows researchers to track the history of each individual cell from its inception in the fertilized egg to its maturity. Molecular biologists such as Brenner have obtained much information from their study of C. elegans. The finds include the identification of some of the biochemicals that trigger unspecialized cells to become the specialized cells of a particular organ or organ system.

Since the early 1960s, C. elegans has become an increasingly popular research subject. At present, more than 200 academic research centers and seven commercial laboratories are engaged in investigating this organism. Study topics include the effects of dietary stress on reproduction, the nature of the aging process, and the genetics of life extension. However, the main focus in most studies is to observe the life stages of a C. elegans cell as the organism matures from egg to adult.

The genetic sequencing of this worm may achieve the goal of identifying the genes responsible for encoding all the enzymes that trigger cellular specialization. Such knowledge would be valuable in establishing the methodology for using embryonic stem cells for human organ repair.

ARABIDOPSIS THALIANA

The humble weed Arabidopsis thaliana thrives on much of the land in Europe and the Middle East. Travelers introduced Arabidopsis to North America many years ago, and it spread there, acquiring such common names as mouse-ear cress and wild mustard. Arabidopsis has no commercial value, although it is occasionally used as an herb. Until the 1940s, the plant was of little concern to botanists or anyone else. Scientific interest in Arabidopsis has increased since then, however, because of some interesting properties. These include the ability to thrive under arid conditions.

In the 1930s, German and Russian geneticists sought a plant that could be used as a standard model in botanical research in much the same way as the fruit fly was used in animal studies. The little wild mustard plant was found to have the advantages of a small number of chromosomes (10), a susceptibility to mutation, and a rapid maturation period, allowing inheritable traits to be studied with little delay. By the 1960s, the plant had become popular among European plant geneticists. When the study of molecular biology expanded in the 1960s and 1970s, *Arabidopsis* was solidly in place as a standard model against which to compare and contrast the properties of other plants.

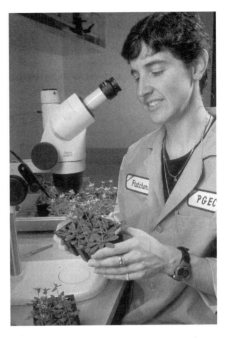

Arabidopsis thaliana, *as a potted plant* (Courtesy of the Agricultural Research Service of the U.S. Department of Agriculture)

Today *Arabidopsis* is used in many lines of research. Plant physiologists are seeking the genes that produce the enzymes and hormones that are active in cell-to-cell communication. Although plants do not have nervous systems, cells in one part of a plant seem to sense what is happening in another part. The stems and leaves of many plants move in response to the Sun's movements across the sky. Researchers want to know how this coordinated action is organized. They believe that the chemicals released selectively by individual cells can signal other cells to join in the coordinated effort. Special organs within the cells use recipes contained in the plant's genes to manufacture these chemicals; therefore, the genes are ultimately responsible for any coordinated action by the plant.

Researchers are also interested in other characteristics exhibited by *Arabidopsis*. Some varieties of *Arabidopsis* thrive in soil that contains more salt than can be tolerated by domesticated crops. Many acres of unusable land could be brought into cultivation if crop plants could be made more tolerant of salty soil. If genetic engineers could identify the genes that give *Arabidopsis* its salt tolerance, those genes could be transferred into the genomes of crop plants such as rice, wheat, and soybeans.

CANIS FAMILIARIS

For many years, dogs (*Canis familiaris*) have been used as test subjects in biomedical research. Today, however, molecular biologists see profound implications in another aspect of dog physiology—the extreme variation among breeds. The variations appear in physical traits such as size and conformation (consider the Mexican hairless and the St. Bernard) and in behavioral tendencies (such as the herding behavior of the border collie and the retrieval behavior of the standard poodle). In spite of such differences, a male and a female of different breeds can produce mixed-breed, fertile offspring.

Careful inbreeding was standardized in the mid-1800s when kennel clubs established formal rules for mating. A dog was recognized as being of a certain breed only if both parents were certified as belonging to that breed. Today, the American Kennel Club recognizes 150 distinct breeds, but dog fanciers around the world claim as many as 300 different breeds.

Inbreeding tends to solidify certain desired characteristics but also does the same for undesired characteristics and some diseases. Cancer provides a case in point. One in three purebred dogs will develop cancer during its life; moreover, the type of cancer tends to be breed specific. Compared to other breeds, boxers and Airedale terriers have twice the number of cases of soft tissue cancers, such as bladder or liver cancer. Cocker spaniels and Boston terriers are most susceptible to breast cancer. Great Danes and Irish setters are prone to bone cancer, and pointers may develop lymph cancer. The specificity of cancer found in different breeds should help medical geneticists identify the mutated or otherwise divergent gene that is shared by the susceptible breed but not found in others. However, it is still too early for disease-specific gene discoveries to emerge from the investigations of the dog genome.

The first rough draft of a dog genome was published in September 2003. This draft was constructed by scientists at Celera Genomics from cells taken from Shadow, a standard poodle. Although many unusual genes were identified in this compilation, the Poodle sequence is far from complete. Meanwhile, 17 academic laboratories worked on a refined draft using a more complete sequence from a boxer named Tasha. The Broad Institute at the Massachusetts Institute of Technology (MIT) published a report on this work in July 2004. The draft has been cross-checked six times and has few gaps.

Preliminary findings in the investigations of the dog genome include the unsurprising fact that dogs have a genetic advantage in their sense of smell. This is derived from their 400

Tasha, the boxer that provided the DNA for the first full genomic sequence from a dog (Courtesy of the National Human Genome Research Institute) or more odor-related genes. Otherwise, the dog genome and the human genome overlap by about 75 percent.

Many dog fanciers, however, were surprised to learn which dog breeds are most closely akin to the gray wolf, their presumed ancestor. The breeds with wolflike genomes include the Afghan hound from the near East, the basenji from Africa, and the Pekingese from China. The wide geographic dispersal of these breeds suggests that their divergence from the ancestral wolf happened over long periods of time and in widely separated locales.

Research has also found that each breed of dog has a distinctive and identifiable genetic fingerprint. After 414 dogs had been genotyped, the investigators organized a blind test to determine whether dog breeds could be accurately identified from their genetic fingerprints. Of the 414 genotyped dogs, participants in the test correctly identified the breeds of 410 of the dogs.

PAN TROGLODYTES

The chimpanzee is widely regarded as the primate whose characteristics are closest to those of human beings. The mass media has proclaimed that the chimp genome and the human genome differ by only 1.5 percent; in other words, they have reported that 98.5 percent of the two genomes are identical. This statement is not exactly true.

First, it is too early to make such a claim. The rough draft of the chimpanzee genome was published in December 2003 by collaborators at Washington University in St. Louis and the Broad Institute at MIT. At present, only the most general comparisons of the total genome have been possible. Recently, however, Japanese researchers conducted additional investigations on a single chromosome. They chose to study the chimpanzee chromosome 22 because it is very similar to the human chromosome 21. When the two DNA sequences were compared, the number of differing nucleotides was indeed about 1.5 percent. This was exactly the same percent that was claimed to represent the difference between the complete genomes of humans and chimps. However, another picture emerged when scientists conducted comprehensive comparisons between specific genes in the human and the chimp chromosomes.

Some 231 chimp and human genes could be directly compared. Of that number, 179 were essentially similar, showing only minor variations such as a substitution in a single nucleotide. Biologists speculate that a variation of a single nucleotide will not make much difference in the protein product. However, 47 genes showed multiple structural changes, indicating that the level of protein functional differences could be as high as 20 percent (five of the genes could not be classified in the test.) That level of variation could readily account for the differences between humans and chimpanzees.

Further analyses have provided the basis for more speculation. For example, the comparison appears to confirm the relative loss of smell sensitivity in humans. On the other hand, humans appear to have gained in the number of genes that relate to both voice control and hearing ability. These differences could help explain human language capabilities. Other differences between humans and the lower primates may be associated with human adaptation to a more varied diet.

Finally, it is important to keep in mind that the human and chimpanzee lineages separated 5 million years ago. Humans are not descended from apes. Both humans and chimpanzees are descended from a common ancestor, and both have been evolving in their own way ever since. In other words, a chimp is just as evolutionarily advanced as a human but has undergone different steps.

The Proteome

Among the many species whose genomes have been sequenced or partly sequenced are the old standard genetic models the bacterium *E. coli* and the fruit fly *Drosophila melanogaster.* The genetic characteristics of these organisms have been studied and documented for the past 90 years. This rich supply of data should provide valuable insights into the field of human genetics and may suggest ways to increase human immunity to various diseases. A full understanding of the medical possibilities, however, will depend on another difficult step. Scientists must first identify and characterize all the proteins that are produced within the human body. This large assembly of proteins is called the proteome, and its study is called proteomics.

Proteins are manufactured in each cell of the body as linear strings or chains of a variety of amino acids, the building blocks of proteins. These strings are called peptide strings or polypeptides. Several transformations take place after the peptide strings are formed. Sections of some chains wind themselves into coils. Other sections develop into ribbonlike structures, and still others remain in the shape of a simple chain. The form taken by any given segment of the peptide string is determined by the types of amino acids that make up that segment and how those amino acids interact. Most completed proteins are made of a combination of the coils, ribbons, and straight chains.

After a segment of protein has assumed one of these intermediate shapes, it folds into a three-dimensional, more rounded form. Interestingly, the specific shapes of both the intermediate forms and the more rounded forms are also determined by the types of amino acids found in each segment. If a protein is to serve as an enzyme, its special variety of amino acids ensures that its shape includes little nooks and crannies. This configuration permits the enzyme to adhere to other chemicals and help in the interactions of those chemicals.

The goal of proteomics is to identify the function of each type of protein produced by a particular species. Research has shown that the human proteome contains at least 50,000 different kinds of proteins. Some are abundant in all cells. These are the thousands of structural proteins that form the cell membrane and the many small substructures within the cell. These substructures include the tiny fibers that support the movement of materials within the cell. Some of the most interesting proteins are scarce in number and rarely present in a cell. Others are infrequently found in cells, and only a few hundred may exist at any one time. Some proteins are transient—or temporary—because they are made for a special

A Three-Dimensional Model of a Protein Molecule

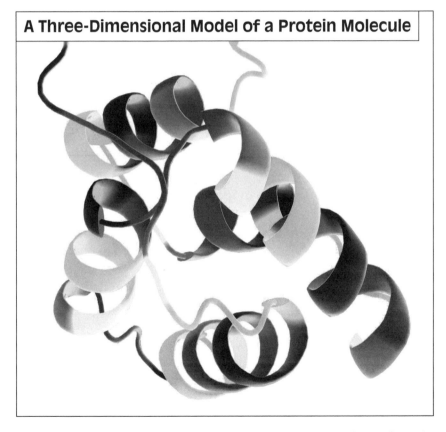

This diagram shows a prototypical protein molecule in the form of a coil, ribbon, and chain model.

purpose. When that purpose is fulfilled, they are broken down and recycled.

The inventory of proteins always varies from organ system to organ system, from cell to cell within an organ, and from time to time in any given cell. The field of protein science deals with an ever-changing array of research possibilities.

The basic thrust of protein research is to isolate, identify, and recognize the function of each type of protein. The investigation usually begins by separating protein molecules by their relative size, electrical characteristics, or both of these classifications. A mixed sample of protein molecules is suspended or dissolved in a solvent, and the procedure called electrophoresis is used to separate the molecules by size and electrical charge. For many years, the next step has been to crystallize the isolated protein molecules. When the crystal is formed, it can be examined by X-ray. When the X-ray image strikes a photographic film, the picture resembles lines of Morse code. The pattern of dark and lighter dots and dashes was, in past years, interpreted by experts using elaborate mathematical procedures. This chore is now often computerized and the component chemicals of each protein molecule can be more quickly analyzed.

In fact, computers can greatly accelerate the whole identification process. For example, different molecules give off different patterns of light when illuminated by a laser tuned to a particular wave length. An array of protein samples can be scanned

A protein crystal formed in ultra-low gravity (Courtesy of the National Aeronautics and Space Administration)

This X-ray machine is used to analyze protein crystals. (Courtesy of Dr. Hwai-Chen Guo, Boston University)

by a photometer—(light meter), and the results plotted on graph paper. The resultant peaks and valleys show the intensity of the radiation and can mark and identify each type of protein molecule.

Even with the improved analytical procedures, further studies on the exact function of each protein type will require years of work. Research has shown that one specific form of protein molecule is necessary to achieve a particular function; however, the precise function of the protein cannot be determined by a simple examination of the form. The protein molecule must be examined in its action mode. To observe this phenomenon, a sample of protein molecules is added to a chemical solution that will activate the molecules. Scientists have been able to determine that the actions of many protein molecules directly affect the actions of other proteins. The final action can be the result of a sequence that progresses from one protein molecule to another.

The ultimate goal of proteomics is not merely to identify all the proteins in each bodily system or simply to see what physical features are engendered by a particular action sequence. An additional goal is to identify the genetic and protein basis for variations in behavior. Researchers have begun this study by using laboratory animals as test subjects in the field of proteomics. In one experiment, two strains of mice were identified: One strain showed hostility when an unrelated mouse was introduced into its cage, whereas the other strain was relaxed when a new mouse was brought into their group. The researchers tentatively identified the contrasting protein sequences found in the two mouse strains. Two different chains of four protein interactions were identified. When the genes that held the codes for these proteins were disabled so that protein production stopped, the behavior of the affected mice changed.

Much time and effort will be needed to discern the proteomic basis for variations in human behavior. This task will be complicated by the fact that most human behavior is learned and therefore subject to social influences. Nevertheless, someday in the future psychological conditions such as emotional mood may be susceptible to modification by genetic or protein interventions. Psychological conditions have been assessed by standardized tests for several years. While exact measurement is elusive and there is some uncertainty about test validities, important decisions hang on these measurement. For example, the effectiveness of psychoactive drugs is assessed by such means. Proteomics will be able to identify the genetic and protein basis for the variations in human biological and psychological characteristics and to use this knowledge to improve human health and well-being.

14
Genetic Screening

Even before the completion of the human genome, scientists had developed techniques for linking genetic patterns to the presence of disease tendencies. The first crude efforts were based on the apparent inheritance of traits from parents and grandparents. Then, the work with fruit fly chromosomes showed that more detailed connections to specific genes could be made. Now, by using techniques similar to genetic profiling, individuals can be screened for tendencies toward particular genetic disorders. These techniques can be used by health care providers as analytic tools alongside standard diagnostic procedures.

Diagnosis and Genetic Screening

The main distinction between screening and diagnosis is the presence or absence of disease symptoms. A diagnosis of a specific illness or condition is made by the health care provider based on the appearance of a pattern of symptoms called a syndrome. These symptoms are identified by such means as medical examinations, X-rays, and patient conferences. After weighing all the facts, the doctor arrives at a diagnosis and then prescribes the most effective treatment for the designated disease.

Screening does not depend on the presence of symptoms and is based on less obvious indicators. Screening comes into play

DNA chromatographs, such as the one shown here, are used to find the markers that are linked to genetic disorders. (Courtesy of the Agricultural Research Service of the U.S. Department of Agriculture)

before the appearance of symptoms and is more predictive in intent. Its usefulness lies in prevention or early treatment or both. However, screening is always ambiguous. The information gained from genetic screening relies on the presence of a unique marker sequence of DNA. The distinctive pattern is found on fragments of DNA that have been severed from their original DNA sequence by the action of a particular enzyme. This marker sequence can identify the victims or potential victims of a particular disease. A healthy person whose DNA fragments show the same pattern is considered susceptible to and a likely candidate for the disease. Nonetheless, some of the people who have the DNA marker that indicates the potential for a specific disease never develop the disease, while others who do not have the marker will develop the disease.

The history of medicine reveals that physicians used a variety of screening tools long before DNA was identified. Information acquired from the older screening methods has the same limitations as the data gained from today's genetic markers. For example, one of the oldest screening procedures is a patient's medical history, which includes questions about the health and life span of close relatives. If these relatives suffered from specific diseases, the patient might have inherited the same problems; therefore, if several relatives died of heart disease, the health care provider will look for signs of coronary weakness in the patient. With or without any confirmation of heart disease, the provider will be inclined to recommend lifestyle changes such as an austere diet and exercise.

Some screening procedures have become so commonplace that no one considers them as unusual or intrusive. Blood and urine samples are taken for laboratory testing prior to a routine medical examination. The blood tests include those for the presence of sugar. A positive result to this blood test might reveal the prospective onset of diabetes, a common, treatable condition. Urine is examined for the presence of protein as an indicator of kidney malfunction, and a more thorough examination might provide the cause and treatment of the problem.

Many illnesses such as acquired immunodeficiency syndrome (AIDS) and sexually transmitted diseases do not exhibit external symptoms until long after a patient has become infected. Effective treatment depends on early detection. Consequently, medical researchers have sought diagnostic tests that are not so dependent on visible symptoms. The Wassermann test for syphilis developed in Germany in 1906 is a blood test that identifies the presence of that sexually transmitted disease.

Screening tests for cancers reveal both the advantages and disadvantages of such procedures. Screening for breast cancer, for example, has become very important, as early detection allows treatment before the cancer can grow and spread to other parts of the body. The principal method of screening is the mammogram or X-ray examination. The X-ray, discovered in 1895 by the German physicist Wilhelm Conrad Roentgen, has been used for medical purposes for more than 100 years, but it is best suited for the examination of hard tissue such as bone. The breast is soft tissue, and early breast X-ray images were very difficult to read. Until the 1960s, mammography was used primarily after a cancerous lump had been detected by a physical examination of the breast. Since the 1960s, technical progress has improved the design of X-ray machines devoted to mammography. Image quality has improved and patient discomfort has been reduced, but many problems are unsolved.

Some cancerous growths remain undetected because mammogram images are often ambiguous. Mammograms, like other screening tools, have a tendency to generate false positives. Patients can be erroneously diagnosed as having cancer or a precancerous condition. Such an error can lead to unnecessary surgery, radiation, or treatment with anticancer drugs. Some medical experts even have reservations about the use of X-rays. They fear that this form of low-intensity radiation may, itself, be harmful.

Additional complications arise from social, economic, and psychological factors caused by cancer detection. The cost and limited availability of mammograms makes this life-saving technique less accessible to poor and minority women. Although breast cancer survival is now relatively commonplace, women continue to fear the negative consequences of cancer detection. The removal of a breast is a real possibility; lump removal, chemotherapy, and radiation therapy are only slightly less threatening. In addition, some therapies lead to temporary bodily weakness and complete or partial hair loss. Thus, detection of cancer or a precancerous condition threatens death or disfigurement, and people tend to avoid such bad news as long as possible.

There are also familial consequences to genetic screening. A mother with breast cancer must decide if and when she should warn her daughters or other female relatives. Since only 10 percent of the women that show the genetic markers actually contract cancer, the results of genetic screening are known to be ambiguous. Her decision must therefore be weighed carefully.

Finally, there is the question of how the patient's genetic screening information will be used by other people. Insurance companies screen some applicants, and health maintenance organizations routinely require extensive patient histories that include the parents' cause of death. Similarly, patients who have specific susceptibilities, such as heart problems, are required to have periodic "checkups," which are actually screening sessions. Likewise, employers typically ask health questions on employment application forms, and workers have been denied employment when those making hiring decisions see a prospective employee as someone who is likely to request extensive sick leave.

Some state laws prohibit exclusion from insurance coverage or jobs based on a previous medical condition or a medical disability. However, some states do not have laws covering genetic discrimination, and there are some serious differences among the states regarding matters such as the maintenance of patient privacy and enforcement provisions. Such lack of consistency among the separate states has led to calls for federal legislation. In 1996, Congress passed the Health Insurance Portability and Accountability Act, which contained provisions assuring the privacy of patients' medical records. Some people saw these as covering genetic screening results along with conventional screening and diagnostic information. Still, some legislators were not satisfied. In 2003, draft bills specifically covering genetic information and discrimination were introduced in both the House of Representatives and the Senate. The Senate bill cleared committee review and was promptly and easily passed. The House bill, however, never cleared committee review and was allowed to die in 2004. Consequently, there are not yet any comprehensive laws against genetic discrimination at the national level.

15
Aging

Mortality is the price of being alive, and humans have long sought ways to avoid paying that price. People have dreamed of magic elixirs, explorers have braved hardships to locate a fountain of youth, and the rich have invested fortunes and undergone pain in an attempt to delay the aging process. Since contemporary society allegedly worships youthfulness, it is no surprise that aging is the focus of well-funded research programs. Much of this research is based on the science of genetics because long life appears to be an inherited trait. If your grandparents lived to an advanced age, you can expect to live beyond the average life expectancy.

Diet

For many years, moral reformers as well as nutritionists have claimed that diet is a key to long life. Health-care specialists advocated dietary restrictions long before the science of genetics was even developed. More recently, research has shown that when animals—ranging from worms to mammals—are fed just enough to sustain their weight, they live longer than those who have been overfed. Such dietary programs proved effective regardless of genetic heritage. On the surface, then, both diet and genetics appear to be causal factors in longevity.

Researchers at Harvard University and at MIT are trying to understand how such dietary restrictions or modifications succeed in prolonging life. Their research has indicated that genetic factors are active in the biological process of nutrition.

Experiments using yeast colonies are of prime importance at both institutions. Scientists have isolated several long-lived families of yeast cells. These cells appear to activate a particular age-retarding gene when their caloric intake is restricted. The researchers now believe that it may be possible to energize this gene by another, not fully researched method. If so, the resultant anti-aging effect could be activated without the loss of vigor or other unwanted side effects that might accompany a severely restricted diet.

The nutritional involvement in activating this possibly life-extending gene and the biochemical consequences that follow are so complicated that the two research teams now disagree about the details. Indeed, the sequence of steps could involve the interaction of DNA, RNA, enzymes, vitamins, hormones, and other biochemicals. Fortunately, the dispute will spur further research.

The purely genetic implications of human longevity exhibit more straightforward linkages than those found in the theories involving the interaction of genetics and nutrition. Studies have demonstrated that one such genetic link is action of insulin and the DNA that holds the code for this hormone. Insulin is a small protein molecule that serves to regulate sugar metabolism. An insulin shortage can cause a surplus of glucose (sugar) in the patient's blood. This condition is known as diabetes, and diabetics often experience extreme weigh loss or gain and circulatory problems and are susceptible to heart disease. Lack of insulin can therefore shorten a lifespan.

A surplus of insulin can be equally debilitating. The excess insulin leads to a condition known as hypoglycemia in which the body suffers from a shortage of blood sugar. The end result can be insulin shock, which produces convulsions, deep coma, and possibly death. The effects of insulin shock are so profound that some patients suffer brain damage or personality change. In the early 1900s, a number of physicians believed that changes in the central nervous system might reduce a drug addict's overwhelming desire for drugs, and overdoses of insulin became a treatment for this problem. During the 1930s and 1940s, severe schizophrenia, the most prevalent psychosis among young people, was also treated by this method. Given the magnitude of adverse side effects—disorientation, decrease in mental ability, depression, and other disabling conditions—it is fortunate that by the mid-1950s, alternative antipsychotic drugs had been developed. Today, insulin is prescribed in carefully regulated dosages exclusively as a treatment for diabetes.

Pigs were among the first sources of medicinal insulin. The problems with animal sources of this hormone led to the first attempts to transfer human genes to microorganisms. (Courtesy of the Agricultural Research Service of the U.S. Department of Agriculture)

In the 1920s, medical insulin was extracted from the pancreatic tissue of animals that had been slaughtered for their meat. However, because the insulin from these sources sometimes induced severe allergic responses, biomedical researchers sought safer methods to treat diabetes. In the 1950s, the British scientist Frederick Sanger described the insulin molecule in detail. By the late 1970s, researchers had identified the gene responsible for the production of human insulin. Scientists soon began producing insulin by inserting the newly identified gene into microorganisms. As the colonies of microorganisms multiplied, the gene was retained by subsequent generations and the production of human insulin was increased. By 1982, commercial quantities of synthetic human insulin were being produced in fermentation vats by huge colonies of yeast cells genetically modified by the human gene. The insulin produced in this manner is more efficient and has far fewer negative side effects than the insulin harvested from animals.

Hormones and Genes

In the early 1980s, researchers studying the biological functions of certain hormones such as thyroid, which controls growth, and estrogen, which controls sexual responses, recognized that some of these hormones carried out functions in the cell nucleus that were different from those they performed in the body of the cell. In the cell body, hormones act on specific proteins and other chemicals to energize chemical reactions such as the production of energy from sugar. In the cell nucleus, however, the hormones interact with the DNA and, in some circumstances, suppress the action of a particular gene. Moreover, in other situations, the hormones may turn on or initiate the actions of a gene. Therefore, a hormone can remotely control the production of enzymes and other proteins.

Recently, insulin was identified as one of these hormones that interact with DNA in the nucleus of a cell. Although self-injection of insulin has become a routine treatment for diabetics, biomedical researchers continue to seek a deeper understanding of the interaction between blood sugar and insulin. Scientists are studying how the human body maintains the energy reserves derived from blood sugar. They are also investigating how such reserves are used when an individual is under stress. All of the studies have led back to the science of genetics, and several of these hormone-DNA interactions have consequences for life expectancy. Among the more important of these processes are the actions of the insulin hormone and other insulin-like molecules. Researchers now believe that the benefits of low-fat or low-carbohydrate diets are strengthened by action of insulin on the genes that enhance longevity. The total process is very complicated and involves genes acting on other genes, hormones functioning as enzymes, and reciprocal controls that can either amplify a gene's expression or suppress it. Intense research is ongoing to obtain practical goals such as the control of obesity, the maintenance of mental abilities, and life extension without painful disabilities and infirmities.

Other Genetic Processes

Each individual's organ systems age at a different rate of speed. In some, the cardiovascular system appears to have a tendency toward early decline. In others, the nervous system seems particularly vulnerable. For still others, the digestive system begins to break down early in maturity. As a consequence, many people face situations in which some bodily functions are impaired while others continue to be robust. Among the most unfortunate individuals are those who suffer from a condition of mental deterioration, such as Alzheimer's disease, at the same time that their other bodily systems are unimpaired.

Humans can also suffer from conditions in which all bodily systems deteriorate at the same time and at an abnormally young age. There are two basic forms of this early aging condition. Medical specialists first described one disorder, called progeria, in the late 1800s. Progeria is very rare and has received little study until recently. Sufferers age very rapidly and usually die at around 13 years of age. Werner's syndrome is a similar condition in which 30- to 40-year-old patients appear to have reached advanced old age. Both conditions are the result of malfunctioning genes. The mutant progeria gene appears to affect a protein that is a part of the cell's nucleus and essential to the cell's health. When the protein is absent, the cell deteriorates rapidly. The critical gene involved in Werner's syndrome supplies the recipe for an enzyme that allows other genes to be copied. Without this critical enzyme, cellular reproduction is impaired.

The physical changes found in the rapid, premature aging process are interesting to biomedical researchers because the patient's accelerated aging allows them to test the patient in a dramatic manner. These diseases also reveal the concrete link between aging and genetics, and their study may generate methods by which to slow the aging process.

Oxygen Poisoning

Early in the Earth's history, the atmosphere contained little or no oxygen. Some single-celled creatures alive today thrive in an oxygen-free environment. These primitive organisms are called anaerobic bacteria (bacteria that need no oxygen). They appear to be remnants of species that evolved when the Earth was young. Oxygen is actually toxic for most such creatures; however, all multicelled organisms require oxygen to live. Some sensitivity to oxygen does remain in modern organisms that thrive on a moderate supply of oxygen. Indeed, oxygen is still poisonous to almost all creatures if the concentration level is raised too high.

A more common form of oxygen poisoning comes from free radicals, or electrically unbalanced molecules such as hydrogen peroxide. Free radicals are produced when animals "burn," or oxidize, the sugar needed to gain the energy to sustain their bodily systems. Free radicals are therefore a product of being alive, and hydrogen peroxide, for example, is found in the bodies of all organisms. In order to balance their electric charge, free radicals seek to gain an electron from the ordinary balanced molecules with which they interact. An illustration of the power of such chemicals is provided when hydrogen peroxide is used as laundry bleach. When a stained article is placed in a mixture of bleach and water, the stain will lighten as the hydrogen peroxide pulls electrons from the electrically balanced chemicals that caused the discoloration. The hydrogen peroxide has disrupted the composition of the molecules that form the stain. A similar but far more complicated situation evolves when hydrogen peroxide grabs an electron from an electrically balanced DNA molecule. This interaction disrupts the composition of the DNA and eventually interferes with its functioning.

Many biologists believe that free radicals gradually destroy some of the crucial molecules in a cell. These free radicals are thought to attack every bodily organ and disrupt DNA molecules, proteins, enzymes, hormones, and the fatty substances called lipids. Tiny mutations can result from these attacks. Fortunately, the mutant substances seldom cause immediate problems because they are confined to the cell in which they occur. As the mutant material accumulates over time, however, the affected cell reproduces inaccurate substances or stops reproducing altogether. Cell after cell in each organ no longer functions fully, and the aging process becomes apparent.

In order to keep bodily organs fully functional, each cell must generate a supply of energy. The chemical process of energy generation is concentrated in the part of each cell called the mitochondrion. This tiny organ not only supplies energy but also contains a supplemental allotment of DNA that is separate from the chromosomal DNA in the cell's nucleus. Some scientists believe that the high rate of energy generation in the mitochondria makes the supplemental supply of DNA more vulnerable to chemical attacks by free radicals.

The aging process caused by free radicals is fought by natural biochemical defenses—the antioxidants produced within each cell. Research has suggested that the effectiveness of these natural antioxidants might be increased by dietary supplements. At present, biomedical interest is centered on dietary antioxidants such as vitamins A and C and the most promising of them, vitamin E. Vitamin E has been effective in sustaining vigor in laboratory animals that are exposed to serious biochemical threats such as cigarette smoke and metallic poisons. Vitamin E evidently blocks the ongoing oxidation damage sustained by most cellular molecules. Unfortunately, the vitamin does not readily penetrate the membrane surrounding the mitochondria and can do little to defend the vulnerable mitochondrial DNA. People with adequate amounts of vitamin E in their diets, however, are likely to suffer less from environmental agents such as cigarette smoke than those whose diets are deficient in vitamin E. Currently, no scientific evidence supports the possibility that vitamin E supplements can extend life.

Cell Death

Biologists and health care providers know that each cell of the body has a programmed life expectancy, called apoptosis. Apoptosis occurs naturally and results when the cell's chromosomes lose their ability to divide and produce replicas of themselves.

Each time a cell divides, the DNA nucleotides must be duplicated to provide a new set of chromosomes. Each nucleotide is a link in the DNA chain and contains a small molecule of a sugar followed by a small molecule of a base and then an atom of phosphorus. To begin the duplication process, a large enzyme called DNA polymerase moves up a portion of the DNA chain and unzips a short strand of nucleotides. As the DNA polymerase moves along each side of the newly unzipped strands, the enzyme copies the nucleotides in its path. The copying stops when the enzyme reaches the phosphorus molecule at the end of the unzipped nucleotides. After the duplication is complete, the unzipped portions of the DNA chain are reunited because their corresponding base elements are naturally attracted to one another. Few lasting mistakes are made during this process because at the instant of their reuniting, each strand of DNA corrects any errors made in the corresponding strand. Indeed, a permanent mistake by the polymerase occurs only about once in every billion nucleotides.

To ensure the reproduction of DNA, the tip end of each chromosome is equipped with a telomere, a thin tail that contains several hundred extra nucleotides. In addition to this safeguard, some cells, such as those that produce eggs or sperm, can recruit the enzyme group called telomerase to replace nucleotides lost from the telomere.

Cancer cells seem to have very effective telomerase enzymes. Normal cells gradually lose portions of the telomere, and when they are used up, the cell can no longer divide. Then the nondividing cell is ready for apoptosis. However, cancer cells are nearly immortal because they are able to retain their telomeres indefinitely. They can go on reproducing until the body of the cancer victim can no longer provide them with nutrients.

Medical researchers such as Elizabeth Blackburn at the University of California at San Francisco are seeking ways to suppress the telomerase in cancer cells. As yet, no one understands exactly how or why cancer cells can produce such effective telomerase. Scientists also hope to comprehend why cells that form into egg and sperm cells have this same capability of longevity without the problem of becoming malignant.

Life expectancy in industrialized countries has more than doubled over the past 200 years. Many of these advances have been achieved by more sanitary living conditions, higher standards for food purity and vastly improved defenses against infectious diseases. Some benefits may also be the result of a reevaluation of dietary practices. Further increases in life expectancy are more likely to result from the ongoing research in genetics, nutrition, and molecular biology. At this time, the future of such investigations is unpredictable.

16
RNA

In the 1980s, the scientific community was taken aback by a discovery in the field of genetics. Researchers had proven that RNA could function as an enzyme. Since the early 1930s, scientists had believed that all enzymes were proteins. They now had to accept the fact that some enzymes are RNA molecules. This concept was very difficult for some in the scientific community.

Enzymes are the action figures of biology. This class of molecule facilitates every biological function from birth to death. For example, various enzymes help the digestive system process food. One of these operates in the stomach and small intestine and, with the help of stomach acids, breaks up the protein molecules in food. Stomach acids alone can perform this function, but, with the help of enzymes, the action accelerates by a factor of more than a thousand. Organic life probably could survive without enzymes, but such life would be primitive and sluggish.

Catalysts and Enzymes

Enzymes are organic catalysts, substances that accelerate chemical reactions but are not changed by the reactions. Catalysis—the action of a catalyst in speeding the rate of a chemical reaction—is the underlying chemical process in enzyme action. This process was discovered long before enzymes were identified because catalysis can occur in flasks and test tubes in a laboratory. Enzymatic action, however, normally takes place within a living cell and is difficult to observe. As early as the 1790s, naturalists noticed that some chemical reactions could be accelerated by the presence of pellets or powder made of metal. Strangely, the metal bits were not chemically changed by the reaction. Even after a new chemical product had been generated, the amount of metal in the laboratory flask was exactly the same at the end of the experiment as it had been at the beginning. By the mid-1800s, the Swedish chemist J. J. Berzelius provided a theoretical explanation for this oddity. He believed that the presence of a catalyst strengthened the electrical attraction between the atoms in the reaction. Although the catalyst itself remained unchanged by the generation of a new chemical product, its presence had sped the assembly of the resultant compound.

As one practical result, the commercial manufacture of sulfuric acid was accelerated by the use of platinum powder as a catalyst. In the late 1800s and early 1900s, many chemical engineers adopted the use of catalysis. Production managers such as those responsible for the production of gasoline from crude oil were among the innovators. The manufacture of commercial chemicals expanded rapidly as catalytic techniques were adopted for many other chemical processes.

In the meantime, some chemists were engaged in the study of fermentation, the transformation of sugar into alcohol. Humans had been using and controlling this process for thousands of years without a full understanding of the procedure. It was not until 1879 that Louis Pasteur, a French chemist and microbiologist, observed that the presence of living cells—yeast cells or those of other microorganisms—is essential to the process of fermentation.

In the late 1800s, the German natural products chemist Eduard Buchner began a new study by collecting the liquid that had been hydraulically squeezed from yeast cakes. After chemically purifying the yeast liquid and combining it with sugar, he observed that the liquid accelerated the process of fermentation. By trial and error, Buchner identified the active chemical in the juice and named it zymase. (*Zym* comes from the Greek word for leaven, the process by which yeast causes bread dough to rise; *ase* is a suffix indicating an enzyme.) Buchner was the first scientist to isolate an enzyme, identify its function, and show that the purified organic material could work outside the confines of a living cell.

Chemists soon suspected that biochemical reactions could be accelerated by a variety of materials derived from living creatures. Research on this hypothesis became the subject of a new scientific study, enzymology. Principal enthusiasts included another German chemist, Leonor Michaelis, and his research associate, the Canadian pathologist Maud Menten. The French scientist Victor Henri also began a major program of research. The results of their studies greatly expanded interest in the field of biochemistry and provided background for the work of biochemist James Sumner, a professor at Cornell University. In 1926, Sumner isolated and purified the enzyme urease. He formed a crystalline residue from this material, tested the residue, and discovered that urease was a protein. Other biochemists were skeptical, and his findings were disputed in the scientific literature; however, a few years later, John Northrop and Wendell Stanley at the Rockefeller Institute of Medical Research in New York isolated another half-dozen enzymes and proved them all to be proteins. The biochemical community was gradually convinced that all enzymes were proteins.

From 1900 to 1975, the field of catalytic chemistry gained basic knowledge and practical applications. By the 1980s, products from catalytic and enzymatic processes had worldwide sales of more than $500 billion per year. The enzyme-based part of this industry has become increasingly important because reactions based on enzymatic catalysis tend to be less environmentally damaging than those based on metal catalysis.

Enzyme Magic

Some of the most interesting enzyme reactions occur within living organisms such as bacteria, which have important commercial uses. Bacterial enzymes, for example, are the chemicals that transform milk into cheese. The natural enzymes in bread mold cells are crucial to the production of penicillin. Pharmacologists are now studying the possibility that these powerful enzymes may provide the next wave of new medicines and other new products.

The development of enzyme studies cemented the idea that protein metabolism is a major biological process. Since 1962, when Francis Crick explained how the DNA code is translated into a recipe for the assembly of proteins, the link between genetics and enzymology has been strengthened. Basic research in this area has included attempts to describe the steps from the transcription of RNA to the production and dispersal of the proteins to their ultimate destination. When completed, such a description will help define the role of the protein molecules in the life of an organism.

One method to pursue this research is to identify the specific gene that contains the recipe for the enzyme in question. Then, that gene can be targeted for suppression. In simple organisms such as bacteria, genes can be selectively "knocked out" or "silenced" by a variety of means. When a gene is silenced, the researchers can then examine the inner workings of the bacterial cell to discern if the absence of the specified enzyme has disrupted an essential biological process. If so, a general idea of the enzyme's function can be determined. Still further study is needed because each biological process might involve a number of distinct stages. Continued experimentation is necessary to pinpoint which enzymes are needed at each stage of the process.

Two independent research teams were pursuing such studies in the late 1970s and early 1980s. Both teams sought to better understand the genetic basis for RNA involvement in ribosomal action of protein production.

A ribosome is a complicated assembly that consists of two relatively large protein composites. One composite incorporates 30 different proteins; the other is composed of 45. The two assemblies attach in much the same way that the back of the left hand can nestle in the palm of the right. The composite ribosome is the site where new proteins are fabricated. Protein production takes place at a point beneath the base of the left hand thumb. Each new protein assembly is composed of long peptide strands. With electron microscopes, scientists can actually see the strands of new protein emerging from the site.

In performing protein production, the ribosome receives messenger RNA (mRNA), decodes it, selects the necessary amino acids brought in by transfer RNA (tRNA), and assembles the proteins. The protein production appears to be aided by another form of RNA. Because of its presence at the crucial site, it is called ribosomal RNA, or rRNA.

One of the research teams studying the role of RNA

This electron microscope is powerful enough to image protein strands as they are formed. (Courtesy of the National Archives Research Service)

molecules in protein production was located at Yale University and headed by the Canadian biophysicist Sidney Altman. Altman was born in 1939 and grew up in Montreal. His parents were immigrants from central Europe who worked in the family grocery business and later shared ownership with other family members. The Altman family had their economic struggles, but they were never impoverished.

As a young person, Sidney was interested in nuclear energy and other practical uses of physics. He also enjoyed studying the lives of the physicists who pioneered the nuclear age. He saw himself as a future physical science student at McGill University in Montreal; however, due to a lucky accident, Altman was accepted at MIT. He found MIT to be mentally and socially stimulating. At the end of four pleasant years, he wrote a well-received senior thesis on nuclear reactions.

After graduation, Altman enrolled in a doctoral physics program at Columbia University, but he soon transferred to the University of Colorado. In 1962, he shifted his interests to biophysics and conducted research on viruses at the Colorado Medical Center. Altman was following the career path of the physicist Max Delbrück, who had conducted notable research on the viruses that attack bacteria. Altman had similar success in this area. After receiving his doctorate in biophysics, he was invited to do postdoctoral study under Crick at Cambridge University. His work there fostered his interest in RNA. After three years of study, Altman isolated a key enzyme in the sequence of chemical steps that leads to the emergence of tRNA. This breakthrough helped initiate his career at Yale University in Connecticut.

At Yale, Altman narrowly focused his research on the role of RNA in the production of proteins. He chemically induced mutations in the DNA of the bacterium *E. coli,* and the mutated genes produced malformed mRNA. Altman and his coworkers then assessed how the structure of the proteins had been affected by the RNA copied from the mutant DNA.

As a side effect of the method, one of the mutations generated an excess of nucleotides in the mRNA molecules. This effect took the form of 50 or more extra nucleotide links at each end of the RNA strand. Altman noticed that a few of these variant RNA strands were repaired spontaneously. Indeed, the malformed RNA resumed its normal form after some unknown enzyme clipped off the excess material. The researchers named the mysterious enzyme ribonuclease P because the excess material had been clipped at the phosphorous (P) junction of the RNA strand.

Sydney Altman (right) received the Nobel Prize in chemistry in 1989 for his discovery of the catalytic properties of RNA. (Courtesy of the Public Relations Office, Yale University)

Their curiosity about this odd phenomenon led the team to try to isolate and analyze the newly identified enzyme. They found that the catalytic function of the enzyme was apparently carried out by a combination of protein and RNA. Altman and his team were hesitant to publish these findings because, at the time (1981), almost every biologist still believed that all enzymes were proteins and that only a protein could be an enzyme. However, further study revealed that the RNA alone could do the repair work. This proved that RNA could function as an enzyme.

Ribonuclease P, the enzyme discovered by Altman and his team, is only 377 nucleotides in length and generates a three-dimensional configuration that is very different from the usual linear RNA strands. This particular RNA molecule includes three large circles joined by double strands. Seven fingerlike elements extend from the circles. Most of the fingerlike elements are made of double strands that may end in small, round knobs. Although the molecule is smaller than a typical protein, it has some of the earmarks of the twisted and folded form of a proteinous enzyme.

The other research team working on RNA variations was located at the University of Colorado at Boulder. The team leader, Thomas Cech, was born in 1947 in Chicago but spent his childhood in Iowa City, Iowa. Cech's grandfather was an immigrant shoemaker from Bohemia; his father was a physician. His parents encouraged scholarship, particularly in the sciences. As a young adult, Cech developed a strong interest in geology and would roam the halls of the Geology Department at the University of Iowa, often talking to the professors about his hobby.

Thomas R. Cech received the Nobel Prize in chemistry in 1989 for his discovery of the catalytic properties of RNA. (Courtesy of the Howard Hughes Medical Institute)

In 1966, Cech entered Grinnell College in the small town of Grinnell, Iowa, about 60 miles due west of Iowa City. There, he majored in chemistry and met his wife-to-be in the organic chemistry laboratory. Cech was attracted to the study of chemical physics and as an undergraduate student qualified for internships at the Argonne National Laboratory near Chicago, and the Lawrence Berkeley Laboratory in California. These experiences directed him away from the study of physics and into the field of biochemistry.

Cech completed his undergraduate degree in 1970 and chose the University of California at Berkeley for his doctoral studies in biochemistry. Cech's thesis adviser was deeply involved in the study of chromosomes and encouraged his graduate student to follow his lead. Cech's decision was the beginning of his lifelong career.

He and his wife moved in 1975 to Cambridge, Massachusetts. She began her postdoctoral studies in chemistry at Harvard University, and he began his at MIT. In 1978, both scholars were offered faculty posts at the University of Colorado at Boulder.

At that time, Cech's main focus was the process by which a gene produced mRNA. He chose the microscopic protozoan *Tetrahymena thermofila* as a test organism. This little creature holds many copies of its rRNA gene in a large, distinctive cell structure called a nucleolus. Since each nucleolus contains about 10,000 copies of the particular gene, Cech found that the separation and purification of the gene proved to be relatively easy.

One of the notable characteristics of the rRNA gene is a long segment that had been uninvolved in the transcription of the code. In other words, the center of the gene contained a long strand of so-called junk DNA. Although not directly related to his main focus, Cech decided to determine how this junk material was eliminated from the rRNA molecule before it took on its function in the ribosome. He and his team members assumed that the removal of the junk material was the work of an unidentified enzyme. This enzyme seemed to clip the RNA strand at the beginning and end of the junk sequence and then rejoin the two pieces of RNA into a single molecule.

Cech used different techniques to find the unidentified enzyme, but it could not be located. While reading about the chemical reactions governing the production of rRNA, he learned that another team had discovered and isolated the same problem segment of junk RNA. Peculiarly, the number of nucleotides of the isolated RNA segment did not match those on the corresponding DNA segment. An extra nucleotide had been added to the RNA piece. No new enzyme could be found to account for this unusual chemical process; however, further investigation revealed that the added nucleotide allowed the former junk RNA to become an enzyme. The catalytic action of the enzyme then allowed that strand of RNA to cut itself loose from the longer strand of operative RNA and reconnect those two pieces. The piece of former junk RNA then folded back on itself to form a closed loop and began to function as an enzyme. The ability to perform in this manner established the fact that the RNA was acting as its own enzymatic catalyst.

Cech and his team, like the team at Yale, were reluctant to publish their findings. In the late 1970s, many in the scientific community were prejudice against the idea that an enzyme could function as both RNA and protein; however, by the early 1980s, the teams were convinced that their discoveries were valid. In 1989, the Noble Prize in chemistry was awarded jointly to Thomas Cech and Sidney Altman.

A Host of Discoveries

After molecular biologists accepted the fact that RNA could function as an enzyme, scientists raced to discover additional roles for catalytic RNA. Researchers soon observed that RNA units were responsible for cutting and splicing the strands of nucleotides that contain the recipe for a protein. They also found that another three, relatively small RNA units were needed for the ribosome to facilitate protein manufacture. Then, more specialized RNA enzymes were discovered. Some of these RNA units add chemical side-chains to protein assemblies to improve their efficiency as enzymes. Still others provide a special capability for the repair of the telomeres that control the reproductive capabilities of chromosomes.

Further research has shown that different types of RNA have crucial functions in the control of genes. One type can silence a particular gene. Another supervises the formation of small, double-stranded RNA segments and then cuts them into two pieces. Each of these segments alone has the capability to silence genes. By 2002, at least 200 different kinds of RNA molecules had been identified. Each has an enzymelike function.

The exact way in which these RNA units interact to regulate gene expression is still mysterious. However, research in the field of genetic science has become a high priority because an understanding of these interactions is vital to the development of treatments for genetic diseases.

An RNA World

The discovery that RNA could act as an enzyme caused a stir among biologists. The finding not only overturned established beliefs but also seemed to resolve some of the problems associated with the origin of life. These problems had always included the possibility that life could arise from nonliving chemicals. Such ideas were complicated by the fact that DNA could not exist without protein enzymes to separate the strands and read the code. However, proteins could not exist without the recipes for their composition held in the DNA. For naturalists, this was a classic chicken-and-egg problem.

Scientists next considered the possibility that, under the right conditions, single strands of RNA might form spontaneously from raw chemicals such as carbon, nitrogen, and phosphorus. Such strands could have the power to reproduce themselves and to evolve into more complicated assemblies.

Such a sequence of events is within the range of possibility; however, many people oppose such ideas. These people totally disagree with those who see RNA as the molecular harbinger of life on Earth. They point out that RNA molecules are quite fragile and might be unable to reproduce—or even survive—outside a cell. They also point out that all cells are composed of proteins that must contain amino acids, an organic product. These and other possibilities make it apparent that advocates of an RNA world are still faced with many uncertainties.

17
Stem Cells

The term *stem cell* was first used by Alexander Maximow, a Russian biologist studying embryology and early development in mammals. In 1909, he authored a scientific paper covering some of the research being done at his laboratory in St. Petersburg. As Maximow studied the blood of his newly born laboratory animals, he observed that some seemingly purposeless blood cells—identifiable by their size and round shape—began to change in form as the animal matured. He realized that the unspecialized cells were transforming into specialized cells as they acquired the characteristic color and shape of blood components such as red blood cells. His paper on this research was presented at a meeting of the Hematological Society in Berlin, Germany. In this paper, he named the newly discovered cells *Stammzelle* in German. He was attempting to convey the idea that these cells were the parents of the specialized blood cells. The term, translated as *stem cells,* continues to be used to designate cells that have no particular function on their own but that engender many different kinds of specialized cells.

Maximow became well known as the coauthor of a comprehensive textbook on the nature of bones and their diseases in the early 20th century, but no one paid much attention to his observations on the mysterious changes that took place in stem cells. Almost 50 years went by before biologists and physicians began to see the medical significance of Maximow's research on the mysterious stem cell.

In the late 1950s, doctors were desperate to discover a treatment for leukemia, the cancer that attacks white blood cells. Leukemia causes white cells, the body's main defense against infection, to undergo periods of uncontrolled growth. This alarming increase in the number of white blood cells deprives red cells, platelets, and other blood components of vital nutrition. As these weakened cells die, the blood gradually becomes unable to sustain the life of the cancer victim. The only available medical response, at that time, was to use powerful drugs, radiation, or both; however, such treatments killed both the weakened normal cells and the deadly cancer cells. Such treatments caused patients to lose their ability to fight infection. Doctors were horrified when recovering cancer patients died from an infectious disease such as pneumonia.

Medical professionals knew that the fatty marrow tissue found in the core of bones produces most white blood cells. In an early attempt to restore healthy blood cell production, physicians fed bone marrow to their patients. Unfortunately, the digestive system broke up the marrow's cell structures, and the marrow tissue could no longer manufacture white blood cells, so administering marrow by mouth did not work.

They next tried to inject bone marrow cells directly into a vein. Ironically, the remnants of the immune system—which had been badly weakened by the cancer and the treatments— acted to reject the marrow cells. Even worse, sometimes the injected cells attacked the patient's body, destroying the last vestiges of its defenses.

Researchers found that by using bone marrow cells from a donor who matched the patient's genetic characteristics would avoid some of the adverse conditions. Indeed, the first successful bone marrow transplants were achieved when the donor was the patient's twin. Other attempts, more or less successful, were achieved when the donor was a close relative.

Medical research soon demonstrated that the problems of incompatibility were basically genetic. Physicians began to look for the unique characteristics of marrow cells that could cause the patient's body to block their acceptance. They soon identified a special family of proteins that were crucial to the immune reaction. These proteins were identified as distinct components of the cell membranes found on bone marrow stem cells. Tests showed that the chemical composition of a cell membrane is "recognized" by antibodies carried by the blood. These antibodies are molecules that act as guardians of the body's defense system and are tailored to attack specific threats. Medical workers have long known that people developed immunity to smallpox if, when young, they are exposed to cow pox, a mild form of the disease. After such exposure, the body can analyze the chemistry of an invading germ, build a specific antibody that recognizes that invader, and then kill that germ whenever it appears. Sometimes, however, the body can mistake a harmless substance for an invader. Allergies can result when pollen grains are identified as enemy organisms.

Similarly, the body can attack donor bone marrow cells if the proteins in the cell membrane trigger a reaction of the patient's antibodies. Fortunately, biochemical tests can now reveal whether the donor's marrow cells contain proteins that are antagonistic to the patient's existing antibodies. Donor's cells are now screened and samples from many prospective donors are tested to determine which cells will have the best possible chance of compatibility with the patient's antibodies.

These advances have led to the idea that bone marrow cells from many volunteers might be screened, sorted, frozen, and stored until bone marrow transplantation was needed. In the 1990s, the resources for treating leukemia patients were further increased when researchers realized that useful stem cells could also be harvested from whole blood. They discovered a rich source of such stem cells in the umbilical cord blood of a new baby. After a voluntary agreement from the newborn's parents, the umbilical cord is not discarded so that the umbilical cord blood can be drawn. The blood cells are then tested for antibody reactions, frozen, and stored. Surgeons can now perform hundreds of stem cell transfusions a month because the test results of blood compatibility are held in a computerized data bank and a match between donor and patient can be located quickly. Although there are now thousands of samples in storage, the supply of stem cells needs to be expanded because satisfactory matches are not always achieved. More donors are needed.

Researchers are also perfecting a new technique that totally avoids the mismatch problem. This approach grew from the frustrations of medical researchers in their inability to control lymphomas, cancers of the lymphatic system. These diseases are particularly dangerous because the lymph system connects all bodily organs and can transport cancerous cells throughout the patient's body. Previously, the common medical response was to use powerful anticancer procedures to eradicate the lymphomas. As in leukemia, such procedures not only kill the cancer cells but also devastate other systems such as blood cell production. Therefore, lymphoma patients, like leukemia victims, need stem cell transfusions. Basic research in the preceding decades revealed that some stem cells are always present in bone marrow and in most bodily tissues. This fact led to a brilliant plan: Physicians began to use stem cells from a cancer victim's own blood to avoid the problem of antibody reactions.

To harvest stem cells from a lymphoma victim, the patient is given medicines that encourage the rapid growth of the body's blood cell reserves. After a few days, the patient's blood is drawn off and immediately run through a special machine that separates out the stem cells. The bulk of the blood is rapidly returned to the patient's body, and the fluid carrying the retrieved stem cells is frozen and stored. When the cancer therapy is completed and the procedure's tendency to kill healthy cells is past, the patient's own stem cells are transfused back into the body and begin to rebuild a healthy supply of blood.

Embryonic Stem Cells

Today, the use of stem cells from bone marrow, from blood from adult donors, or from umbilical cord blood that is volunteered by a newborn's parents is an accepted, uncontroversial procedure. There is, however, another kind of stem cell that appears to have great medical potential but raises serious social and moral questions. These are the embryonic stem cells.

In the 1950s, when scientists first noted the presence of stem cells in many bodily organs, most of their basic research was conducted with laboratory mice. The reproductive systems of both male and female mice were studied to determine

Embryonic stem cells in the process of transforming into nerve cells
(Courtesy of Alexander Muraskov, East Carolina University School of Medicine)

the presence of stem cell populations. Scientists were struck by the relative abundance of stem cells in the umbilical cords of newborn mice. This fact suggested that the early stages of fetal development might produce rich sources of stem cells. In the 1980s, researchers discovered this plentiful source in the earliest embryonic stage of laboratory mice. Specifically, the potentially multipurpose cells were found to be concentrated in the embryonic blastocyst, a spherical assembly of cells that is formed a few days after the fertilized egg begins to develop. This microscopic ball—much smaller than a pinpoint—contains a supply of pure stem cells. In 1984, samples of such cells were extracted from mouse blastocysts and kept alive on a nutrient base. The cells soon began to multiply, and the supply could be maintained and even expanded.

The great advantage of embryonic stem cells is that they have no assigned function. Bone marrow stem cells will readily become functioning white blood cells but are unlikely to replace any other type of body tissue. Stem cells from blood, even umbilical cord blood, also turn into blood cells. Embryonic stem cells, however, can be used to rebuild any organ system, including the nervous system and the brain. In the early 1990s, Japanese scientists were able to direct embryonic stem cells from one mouse to form new nerve cells in the body of another mouse.

In 1998, two separate teams of researchers—one at the Johns Hopkins University in Baltimore, Maryland, and the other at the University of Wisconsin at Madison—succeeded in making human embryonic stem cells grow and reproduce on an artificial medium. Each team used a slightly different technique from those employed by the mouse stem cell researchers, but both teams achieved human stem cell multiplication. To begin the research, patients at a fertility clinic donated human blastocysts. These tiny cell assemblies were removed from the woman's body by simple suction. The blastocysts were opened, and with the aid of micro-instruments, the stem cells

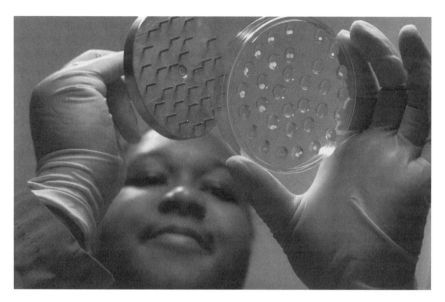

As a technique to help embryonic stem cells multiply, they are inoculated onto a Petri dish. (Courtesy of the Agricultural Research Service of the U.S. Department of Agriculture)

were removed. All the harvested stem cells from a single donor were placed on a sterile nutrient bed in a laboratory dish and allowed to multiply.

After a few generations, some of the cells took on the key chemical characteristics that signify potential skin cells or sense organs such as eyes. Other cells showed biochemical attributes that indicated prospective internal organs such as the liver or the heart. Still other cells seemed destined to become parts of the spinal column. Investigators found that some preliminary specialization occurs spontaneously but that more specific specialization can be induced by adding certain enzymes or stimulants to the growth medium. Hormones may also influence the fate of the embryonic cells.

The microscopic study of early embryonic development will aid gynecologists and obstetricians in understanding the sequence of events that leads to the formation of the amnion, the tissue envelope that encloses the fetus. With the ability to observe and understand the changes that occur as stem cells multiply, other early life stages can now be studied more precisely.

Long-range goals include the use of embryonic stem cells in transfusions and implantations to replace damaged body tissues. Possibly, stem cells could supplant deteriorated muscle cells so that full muscle function would be restored, or they could replace the brain cells destroyed by Parkinson's disease. Indeed, doctors look forward to the time that they can repair all severely damaged bodily organs.

Some people, however, see a grave problem in the harvesting of embryonic stem cells. To retrieve the cells, the blastocyst must be removed from the woman's body and opened by a microscopic instrument. When this technique is used, the blastocyst can no longer survive. Many see the procedure as the equivalent of an early-stage abortion and raise profound moral objections. Ethical, societal, and scientific considerations will need to be resolved before unhindered scientific research and medical developments can proceed.

18
Future Prospects

There are many circular patterns of cause and effect in genetics. Some of the outcomes with respect to the final production of structural proteins, such as those in muscle cells, or hormones, such as insulin, can be the result of the interaction of a dozen or more enzymes—each of which is the product of a separate gene. Sometimes genes that act together are located adjacent to one another on a single chromosome; however, that rule is not always followed. In fact, the enzymes in some of the complicated arrangements may be crafted from genes located on totally different chromosomes. These patterns of interaction need to be described and explained.

An intriguing question in genetics is, Why have humans retained so much DNA that has no apparent use? It takes energy from the cell to construct all the DNA every time the cell divides. It is puzzling that so much energy is wasted in fabricating seemingly useless DNA.

Another mystery that will require many years to solve is the way the genes work during the growth and development of individuals. For example, there are at least six genes that direct the production of various types of hemoglobin. Some of these genes are active in the embryo before birth. Others start to work during childhood. Others come on-line at puberty. Clearly, there are slightly different bodily needs at each of these stages of growth, but what triggers the start-up of one set of genes and the closing down of the other set? To generalize, what turns these genes on and off in the different organs and at the different stages of life?

It is not far-fetched to assert that all disease has a genetic link. That assertion is supported by the fact that some people are naturally immune to some diseases. Specifically, there is no disease to which everyone is susceptible. For example, when the various plagues struck in Europe during the Middle Ages and intermittently over the following centuries, everyone who was exposed did not become ill. Some had a natural immunity to the disease that was killing half their friends and neighbors. Similarly, it is now known that some people are immune to the human immunodeficiency virus (HIV) that causes AIDS. They can be repeatedly exposed to the virus and nothing happens.

The immune response is a genetic mechanism. In particular, natural immunity—that which is present before the individual is ever exposed to the pathogen—is based on the presence in the body of cells and the enzymes carried by cells that can defeat a given invader.

Genetics could feasibly give to human society the complete control over the immune system. Such control would allow people to be disease free for their entire lives. Such control would allow organ transplants to take place that are now either very risky, very temporary, or simply impossible. Organ transplants from non-human animals could be possible if total control over the immune system was achieved.

Work in this arena is moving ahead for food crop plants. For example, some of the genes in wheat that provide this plant with immunity

An electron micrograph of HIV infectious agents (Courtesy of the National Library of Medicine)

from various diseases have already been identified. These genes have been inserted in wheat seeds. Similar progress is being made with a variety of noncrop plants and domestic animals. The bridge from here to humans is a long one. Even though some immunity genes are present already in some humans, it will be difficult to incorporate such genes in everyone—but not impossible.

Even though progress toward control of the human immune reaction will be slow, other lines of research in the field are making good headway. The production of human hormones and enzymes in nonhuman organisms such as sheep or bacteria is well established.

Soy plants that have been given extra resistance to disease by gene transfer (Courtesy of the Agricultural Research Service of the U.S. Department of Agriculture)

Likewise, the identification of the malfunctioning genes that are responsible for many human ills is rapidly expanding. All in all, genetic science has led to better food crops and better methods of medical diagnosis. Of possibly greater importance in the long run, genetic science has vastly expanded human understanding of basic biological processes.

Glossary

adenine A nitrogenous base that is one part of the base pair adenine-thymine (AT).

allele The genetic location for a particular trait, such as eye color.

allogenic Characterized by variation in alleles among members of the same species.

amino acids The relatively small carbon-based molecules containing nitrogen that are combined to form proteins.

antibiotic A substance that interferes with the growth or the reproduction of microbes.

antibody A protein generated by blood cells that enter the bloodstream and combat or neutralize antigens.

antigen A particular foreign material in the body that stimulates the immune system to defend itself by producing materials called antibodies.

apoptosis The process by which a cell undergoes death due to a built-in program. The body's normal method of disposing of damaged, unwanted, or unneeded cells.

autosome A chromosome not involved in gender determination. Twenty-two pairs of human chromosomes are autosomes; in other words, in the human total of 46 chromosomes, only the X and Y chromosomes are not autosomes.

bacteria Very small, single-cell creatures that are ever present in soil, water, air, and living plants and animals. Many thousands of species of bacteria exist. Some species are helpful to humans, most are neutral, and some are harmful.

base pair (bp)   The two bases that join to form the connections between the strands of nucleic acid in a DNA molecule.

base sequence   The order of the nucleotides in a DNA molecule.

behavioral genetics   The study of genes that might influence behavior.

biochemistry   The study of the chemicals that are used by living creatures.

blood type   One of four basic categories of human blood, determined by proteins on the surfaces of red blood cells. Blood types are A, B, AB, and O.

cancer   A group of conditions characterized by rapid growth of body cells beyond the normal needs of tissue replacement. These cells often form lumps or tumors and tend to destroy healthy tissue.

carcinogen   A physical or chemical factor that contributes to the development of a cancer.

cell   The basic structural of all living creatures except viruses. Each cell is made of a watery substance, called protoplasm, surrounded by a thin wall called a membrane.

chimera   An organism that contains cells or tissues from more than one genotype.

chromatography   The separation of different substances in a mixture due to some physical property of each substance, such as the size of the different molecules.

chromosome   A DNA or RNA molecule in the cell that contains all or most of the genetic information of the cell.

clone   An individual organism or cell genetically identical to another, both of which are produced from a common ancestor by asexual means.

codon   A sequence of three bases on a strand of DNA that designate a particular amino acid in the construction of a protein.

complementary DNA   DNA that is synthesized from a messenger RNA template.

conserved sequence   A sequence in a DNA molecule that has remained essentially unchanged throughout the evolutionary history of an organism.

crossbreeding   Mating between two organisms of the same species that have different lineages or are of different varieties within the species.

crossing over   The exchange of corresponding segments between paired chromosomes.

cytoplasm   The contents of a cell outside the nucleus.

cytoplasmic trait   A genetic trait associated with a gene from a strand of DNA found outside the nucleus.

cystic fibrosis   A genetic disease whose symptoms are lung congestion and digestive problems. The gene for this disease is recessive, so a victim must inherit the same defective gene from both parents.

cytosine   A nitrogenous base that is one part of the base pair guanine-cytosine (GC).

deletion   The loss of one part of the DNA in a chromosome (e.g., by mutation), possibly leading to disease or an abnormal condition.

deoxyribose   A small sugar molecule that is one component of a nucleotide in the DNA chain.

digestion   The process by which complex materials are broken down into smaller molecules.

diploid   A full set of genetic material consisting of paired chromosomes, one-half coming from each parental set. The human diploid consists of 23 pairs (46 chromosomes).

DNA   An abbreviation of deoxyribonucleic acid, the molecule of heredity that holds the instructions for the manufacture of proteins by the machinery of a living cell.

DNA sequence   The order of the base pairs, whether in a DNA fragment, a gene, an intact chromosome, or an entire genome.

domain   A particular portion of a protein with its own particular role or function. The aggregate set of the domains of a protein determines its overall function.

dominant gene   The gene that is more likely to be expressed when two genes compete to direct the same trait.

double helix   The spiral formed when two strands of nucleic acid are bonded together by base pairs.

Drosophila melanogaster   The small fruit fly (about 0.12 inches, or 6 mm, long) used to study genetics and developmental biology.

egg   The reproductive cell produced by a female animal.

electron microscope   A device that uses a flow of electrons to form images that are greatly magnified.

electrophoresis   A method for separating sets of large molecules from a mixture of similar molecules that uses the size of the molecule and its electrical polarity.

embryology   The study of the early stages of life.

embryonic stem cells   Immature cells that can multiply for many generations and can be induced to take the form of different specialized cells, such as skin cells or nerve cells.

enzyme   A protein molecule that promotes chemical reactions without being changed in the process; an organic catalyst.

epistasis   A condition whereby one gene prevents the expression of another gene.

Escherichia coli   A common bacterial species that is used frequently in genetic research.

eugenics   The study of means to improve a species by selective breeding. (Usually the term refers to human breeding practices.)

expression   The production of proteins directed by a gene.

fermentation   The process by which microbes change the chemical makeup of a substance. Commonly, the action of yeast on sugar to produce alcohol.

fertilization   The process by which a male reproductive cell merges with a female reproductive cell to produce a cell that can grow into a mature creature.

fission   The process of cell division. In the case of one-celled creatures, each of the two resulting cells forms a new individual.

functional genomics   The study of genes, their resultant proteins, and the roles played by the proteins in the body's biochemical processes.

gamete   A mature reproductive cell (such as a sperm cell) with a half-set (haploid) of chromosomes (23 for humans).

gene   The part of the chromosome that determines a single trait. One gene carries the plan for one protein molecule.

gene expression   The process by which the gene's coded information is converted to vital molecules, such as proteins and enzymes.

gene mapping   Determining the relative locations of genes on a chromosome.

gene therapy   Treatment of a disease by the introduction of a new gene into a cell to replace one that is missing or malfunctioning.

genetic disease   A condition caused by the failure of a gene to function properly.

genetic engineering   The manipulation of the heredity of a given creature by deleting genes or introducing new genes into its cells.

genetic marker   A gene or other notable portion of DNA whose influence on bodily functions can be tracked.

genetic polymorphism   Differences in individuals (such as eye color) that is due to differences in their DNA sequences.

genetic screening   Testing people so as to identify individuals with a high risk of having a specific genetic disorder.

gene transfer   The incorporation of new DNA into an organism's cells as in gene therapy.

genome   The complete set of genes for a given species.

genotype   The genetic composition of a particular person or organism.

guanine   A nitrogenous base that is one part of the base pair guanine-cytosine (GC).

haploid   The state of a reproductive cell having half the number of chromosomes required to produce a new individual.

helix A spiral shape, twisted so that the distance between twists is constant.

hemizygous Having only one copy of a particular gene. In humans, males are hemizygous for the genes found on the Y chromosome.

heredity The transmission by living creatures of their traits to their offspring.

highly conserved sequence A DNA sequence that is very similar across several species.

homeobox A short sequence of nucleotides that appears in several genes in several species. The sequence might be the key to understanding why and how particular genes are active during particular stages of maturation.

homology Similarity in DNA sequences between individuals.

hormone A substance produced by bodily organs that regulates the functions of other organs.

hybrid The result of crossbreeding two varieties within the same species.

hybridization Specific to molecular biology, the joining of two complementary strands of nucleic acid by base pair linkages.

incubate To provide warmth and maintain a temperature that is ideal for growth.

informed consent The commitment of an individual to participate in a therapeutic procedure after being thoroughly informed of the possible consequences.

inoculate To implant microorganisms or infectious material into a living creature or onto a substance that will permit the microorganisms to grow.

insertion A segment of DNA that is not a normal portion of a gene and may upset the gene's function.

insulin A hormone formed by the pancreas that regulates the way in which sugar is used to fuel the bodily processes.

interbreeding See **crossbreeding.**

interferon An antibody produced to combat a virus infection.

linkage   The distance between two or more markers in a chromosome that can be an indication of the probability that genes in the enclosed interval will be inherited as a set.

meiosis   The process of two cell divisions with only one cycle of chromosome reproduction, resulting in four reproductive cells containing a single set of chromosomes instead of two sets, as found in most cells.

membrane   A thin, soft, and pliable skin or covering of a biological unit, such as a cell, or a structure, such as an organ.

messenger RNA (mRNA)   The RNA that serves as a template for protein synthesis.

metabolism   The complete range of chemical processes that sustain life.

microbe   A living creature that cannot be seen with the naked eye. Commonly, a single-celled creature.

mitochondria   Small structures within the cytoplasm of a cell that provide sites for the release of energy within the cell. These structures can also contain strands of DNA independent of the nucleus.

mitosis   Cell division that leads to two complete daughter cells.

mutation   Broadly, a change within a single generation in a trait or characteristic that is commonly expressed by a given species.

natural selection   The manner by which those traits that support individual survival and reproduction are retained by a species. The mechanism of evolution proposed by Charles Darwin.

nitrogenous base   One of the slightly alkaline submolecules that pair to form the connections between the strands of a DNA molecule.

nuclear transfer   The insertion of the nucleus from one cell into another cell (e.g., an egg cell) from which the original nucleus has been removed. A step in the production of a clone.

nucleic acid A chain of nucleotides which in turn are units made up of a sugar, ribose or deoxyribose, and a slightly alkaline submolecule known as a base, such as adenine.

nucleolus A small structure within the nucleus of a cell that contains high concentrations of RNA.

nucleotide The unit formed by one sugar molecule, phosphoric acid, and a nitrogenous base.

nucleus A central and usually the largest structure within a cell and which contains most of the cell's DNA.

oligogenic Of a trait, produced by two or more genes working together.

oncogene A gene that is capable of causing normal cells to become cancerous.

open reading frame The sequence of DNA or RNA located between a gene's start code and stop code.

osmosis The movement of a liquid through a membrane from a more concentrated solution to a less concentrated solution.

ovum An unfertilized egg cell.

pancreas A gland that secretes digestive fluids into the small intestine and the hormone insulin into the bloodstream.

phage A virus that invades bacteria.

phenotype The characteristics of an organism that are not exclusively genetic (e.g., learned skills).

plasmid A circular strand of DNA found mainly in single-celled organisms that have no nucleus.

polymerase An enzyme that promotes the assembly of nucleic acids on a selected or designed template.

polymerase chain reaction (PCR) The actual production of DNA sequences.

polymorphism Variation among individuals due to genetic differences.

probe A DNA or RNA template having a radioactive label; used to identify a complementary sequence.

prokaryote A cell without a nucleus (e.g., a bacterium).

protein A relatively large carbon-based molecule that is an assembly of amino acids. Such molecules always contain nitrogen and often other elements such as sulfur or phosphorus.

proteomics The study of all the proteins encoded by the genome.

protoplasm The clear fluid that contains proteins, fats, and minerals and that makes up the bulk of all living cells.

recessive gene A gene that remains dormant when in competition with a gene that directs an alternative version of the same trait.

recombinant DNA DNA that includes genes from two or more different species; usually created through laboratory techniques.

recombinant DNA molecule One of a set of DNA molecules that are joined together by technical rather than natural means.

recombination The regrouping of genes along a DNA molecule, which occurs naturally during meiosis or artificially through laboratory techniques.

restriction enzyme A protein that recognizes specific short DNA sequences and cuts the DNA at that spot.

restricted fragment length polymorphism (RFLP) Variations between individuals with respect to the pattern of fragments of DNA cut by enzyme action.

RNA An abbreviation of ribonucleic acid, the molecules that help translate genetic information in DNA into proteins and that exist in three varieties: messenger RNA (mRNA), which carries the information from a gene within the cell nucleus into the cell body; transfer RNA (tRNA), which captures nucleotides and delivers them to a ribosome; and ribosomal RNA (rRNA), which provides the inner workings of a ribosome.

sequencing The determining of the order of the nucleotides along a strand of DNA or RNA.

sex-linked characteristic A trait that is carried by a gene located on one of the chromosomes associated with gender determination (in humans, the X or Y chromosome).

sickle-cell anemia A hereditary disease in which defective red blood cells impair circulation.

single nucleotide polymorphism A sequence variation (e.g., the replacement of one nucleotide) in a gene or RNA strand, which can cause an abnormality such as sickle-cell anemia.

species A group of similar creatures that can interbreed and produce fertile offspring.

structural genomics The study of the structural form of proteins using both laboratory techniques and computer simulations.

suppressor gene A gene that can inhibit the action of another gene.

syndrome The set or pattern of symptoms that indicate that a specific disease is present.

telomere A specialized structure at the end of a chromosome that apparently helps control the integrity of the DNA molecule that makes up the chromosome.

thymine A nitrogenous base that is one part of the base pair adenine-thymine (AT).

thyroid gland A large gland located in the neck, which produces the hormone that regulates growth and energy utilization.

transcription The fabrication of a molecule of messenger RNA that copies the sequence of bases from the DNA of a gene.

transgenic Of an organism, containing genes from another species.

tumor A swelling or lump of tissue, often an abnormal growth.

X and Y chromosomes The two human chromosomes that carry the genes that determine gender. Females have two X chromosomes; males have one X and one Y.

zygote The cell formed by the union of the male and female reproductive cells.

Further Reading

Aaseng, Nathan. *Genetics: Unlocking the Secrets of Life.* Minneapolis, Minn.: Oliver Press, 1996. The lives and scientific accomplishments of the pioneers of genetics and molecular biology are presented in sequence, beginning with Charles Darwin and proceeding through to Ananda Chakrabarty, the developer of crude oil–consuming bacteria that have been used to control spills from tankers.

Ackerman, Jennifer. *Chance in the House of Fate.* Boston: Houghton Mifflin, 2001. The main emphasis is the genetic heritage that is substantially shared among Earth's many species—even between plants and animals. The author covers the basics of genetics with a deftness that makes the book highly readable.

Bishop, Jerry E., and Michael Waldholz. *Genome.* New York: Simon and Schuster, 1990. This book provides a detailed discussion of the possible commercial consequences of the Human Genome Project, with an emphasis on medical diagnosis of genetic diseases.

Bornstein, Sandy. *What Makes You What You Are.* Englewood Cliffs, N.J.: Messner, 1989. This book provides a thorough discussion of the way in which traits are inherited. It covers the Mendel research and the modern theories of the functions of DNA and RNA in the cell. It is suitable for a wide range of readers.

Burnham, Terry, and Jay Phelan. *Mean Genes: From Sex to Money to Food, Taming Our Primal Instinct.* Cambridge Mass.: Perseus Publishing, 2000. This book attempts to put human evolution and the problems of modern humans in a genetic framework, showing why it is sometimes so hard to be good.

Darling, David. *Beyond 2000: Genetic Engineering.* Parsippany, N.J.: Dillon Press, 1995. Basic cell biology, genetic diseases, the Human Genome Project, and cloning are topics covered in an informal manner by this book. The treatment is very straightforward and readily understandable, and the illustrations are particularly vivid.

Fridell, Ron. *DNA Fingerprinting: The Ultimate Identity.* New York: Franklin Watts, 2001. The author reviews the origins of forensic genetics and brings the reader up-to-date with applications to wildlife conservation and food inspection.

Gee, Henry. *Jacob's Ladder: The History of the Human Genome Project.* New York: Norton and Co., 2004. Rather advanced, this book ties together genetics, embryology, and evolution in a common framework and then proceeds to show how a team of genes rather than a single gene can work to advance the development of the individual.

Gutnik, Martin J. *Genetics: Projects for Young Scientists.* New York: Franklin Watts, 1985. The various projects described in this book include repetitions of some of the classic experiments with plants and fruit flies. Step-by-step instructions are provided. Some of the projects would be suitable for presentation at a science fair. In addition, the book contains a general review of genetic science and some of the prospects for medical applications.

Hamer, Dean H., and Peter Copeland. *Living with Our Genes: Why They Matter More Than You Think.* New York: Doubleday, 1998. The emphasis is on the role of the genes in interaction with environmental and cultural factors in determining lifestyle choices.

Ingram, Ray. *Twins.* New York: Simon and Schuster, 1989. Discussion of the processes by which twins come about in a useful way that illuminates the mechanisms of inheritance of biological characteristics. Curiosity about twinning can be used as a motivation for scientific study. This book also covers the logic of scientific research in a discussion of the prevalence of myths and spurious "facts" about twins.

Jackson, John F. *Genetics and You.* Totowa, N.J.: Humana Press, 1996. The focus of this book is on the medical problems that arise from the inheritance of faulty genes from one's forebears. It covers the diagnosis, explanation, patient counseling, and both current treatments and possible future options.

Jones, Steve. *Y: The Descent of Man*. Boston: Houghton Mifflin, 2003. The author explains such mysteries as male pattern baldness and variations in sperm count by defining the role of the male (Y) chromosome and discussing how and why it carries so many unfortunate properties.

Panno, Joseph. *Aging*. New York: Facts On File, 2004. While there are many different scientific views on the aging process, advances in molecular biology and genetics have taken us to the edge of a new understanding and the possibility of at least partial control of human aging. The progress in science will raise many ethical, social and economic issues.

————. *Stem Cell Research*. New York: Facts On File, 2004. The author shows why stem cells are necessary if repairs are to be made to those bodily organs such as the heart and liver that have little if any regenerative capabilities.

Ridley, Matt. *Genome: The Autobiography of a Species in 23 Chapters*. New York: Perennial Press, 2000. The author steps from chromosome to chromosome, picking highlight genes at each step. This approach allows the coverage of all facets of genomics in a way that sustains the reader's interest.

Silverstein, Alvin, Virginia B. Silverstein, and Laura Nunn. *DNA*. Brookfield, Conn.: Twenty-first Century Books, 2002. This book covers basic science in a comprehensive way and goes on to tackle the ethical and moral issues that are raised by modern molecular biology.

Yount, Lisa. *Genetics and Genetic Engineering*. New York: Facts On File, 1997. A look at the history of genetics through the stories of 10 major scientists; written for young adults.

Web Sites

The following list contains a sample of sites on the World Wide Web that provide up-to-date information on genome research, genetics and longevity, genetic screening, genetic therapies, newly discovered properties of RNA, and stem cell research. Owing to the nature of the Internet and the rapid changes that occur there, they may have changed since this book was published. If so, the site's name or topic can be used as a search term that should lead to alternative sites and links to other relevant information.

Academic Research Organizations

A multidisciplinary arrangement at Harvard University is the Bauer Center for Genomics Research. URL: http://www.cgr. harvard.edu.

The Broad Institute staff members develop research procedures and instruments for genomic studies. URL: http://www.broad. mit.edu.

In Holland, one of the major research efforts is provided by the Evolutionary Genetics Group. URL: http://www.rug.nl/biologie/ onderzoek/onderzoekGroepen/evolutionarygenetics.

A key member of the cooperative network of research centers around the globe is the Kazusa DNA Research Institute in Japan. URL: http://www.kazusa.or.jp/en.

One research center that tries to bridge the gap between basic science and applied technologies is the Stanford Genome Technology

Center in the Department of Biochemistry at Stanford University School of Medicine. URL: http://www-sequence.stanford.edu.

Activist Organizations

The Alliance for Bio-Integrity is a group with headquarters in Iowa that argues against the development of genetically engineered crops and animals. URL: http://www.biointegrity.org.

The Center for Genetics and Society is an organization that seeks open public review of advances and developments in genetic technology. URL: http://www.genetics-and-society.org.

The Institute of Science in Society sounds a cautionary note about all efforts to modify genetically organisms of any kind. URL: http://www.i-sis.org.uk.

Scientists and Engineers for Change is a new group that is trying to bring scientific findings into the political process. URL: http://scientistsandengineersforchange.org.

Commercial Organizations

Affymetrix provides analytic services, such as the search for genes related to cancer. URL: http://www.affymetrix.com.

Celera Genomics is a major contributor of data to the effort to sequence the human and other genomes. URL: http://www.celera. com.

Cord Blood Registry provides clients with the capability to extract, freeze, and store stem cells from the umbilical cord. URL: http://www.cordblood.com.

Elixir Pharmaceuticals is a company that is dedicated to finding ways to forestall aging. http://www.centagenetix.com.

Integrated Analytical Solutions offers customers the capability to perform protein sequencing. URL: http://www.ias-lcms.com.

Lark Technologies provides customers with molecular biology services and DNA sequencing data. URL: http://www.lark.com.

Government and International Organizations

The staff at the Centers for Disease Prevention and Control seeks to make all citizens aware of the promise and the problems of genetics in the area of public health. URL: http://www.cdc.gov/genomics/public.htm.

The Department of Energy works in partnership with the National Institutes of Health on the Human Genome Project. The project's home page is http://www.doegenomes.org.

The Genome Group is a research team supported by the U.S. Department of Energy at the Brookhaven National Laboratory. The team is exploring plant genomes and the proteins at work in plants and animals. URL: http://www.genome.bnl.gov.

The researchers in the Human Genetics Lab at the Jawaharlal Nehru Centre for Advanced Scientific Research, Bangalore, India, are working on the genetics of diseases of the nervous system. URL: http://www.jncasr.ac.in/anand.

The National Institutes of Health hosts a site for the National Human Genome Research Institute. URL: http://www.genome.gov.

The Sanger Institute is part of the Wellcome Trust, a major source of philanthropic support for medical research in Britain. Staff conducted the early follow-up studies on RNA and protein sequencing and have made major contributions to the characterization of the human genome. URL: http://www.sanger.ac.uk.

Index

Italic page numbers indicate illustrations.